SADLIER
FAITH AND
WITNESS

CREED

A Course on Catholic Belief Part I

Norman F. Josaitis, S.T.D.

Rev. Michael J. Lanning, O.F.M.

William H. Sadlier, Inc.
9 Pine Street
New York, New York 10005-1002
http://www.sadlier.com

Acknowledgments

Scripture selections are taken from the *New American Bible* Copyright © 1991, 1986, 1970 by the Confraternity of Christian Doctrine, Washington, D.C. and are used by license of the copyright owner. All rights reserved. No part of the *New American Bible* may be used or reproduced in any form, without permission in writing from the copyright owner.

Excerpts from the English translation of the *Catechism of the Catholic Church* for use in the United States of America, Copyright © 1994, United States Catholic Conference, Inc.—Libreria Editrice Vaticana. Used with permission.

Excerpts from the English translation of *The Roman Missal* © 1973, International Committee on English in the Liturgy, Inc. (ICEL); excerpts from the English translation of *Rite of Penance* © 1974, ICEL; excerpts from the English translation of *A Book of Prayers* © 1982, ICEL; excerpts from the English translation of *Order of Christian Funerals* © 1985, ICEL. All rights reserved.

English translation of the Our Father, Apostles' Creed, and Nicene Creed by the International Consultation on English Texts, (ICET).

Act of Faith, Act of Hope, Act of Love from *Handbook for Today's Catholic* © 1994, Liguori Publications, are used with permission. All rights reserved.

The Mysteries of the Rosary, *Catholic Household Blessings and Prayers* © 1988 United States Catholic Conference, Washington, D.C. Used with permission.

Cover Illustrator: Diane Fenster

Jim Saylor
Photo Editor

Lori Berkowitz
Assistant Photo Editor

Cover Photos

Art Resource: back cover, center. *The Crosiers/* Gene Plaisted, OSC: front cover, bottom left; front cover, top right. *Anne Hamersky:* back cover, top left.

Photo Credits

Adventure Photo and Film: 29; Pressenbild: 37; Steven Alvarez: 54.
Art Resource/ Erich Lessing: 91; Scala: 68, 92; Giraudon: 108.
John Brandi, Jr.: 100.
Myrleen Cate: 59.
Catholic News Service/ Lisa Kessler: 34.
Cleo Photography: 98.
Carr Clifton: 64–65 center, 86.
Comstock: 118.
Corbis: 100–101.
The Crosiers/ Gene Plaisted, OSC: 18, 116, 117.
Envision, Inc./ Norman Isaacs: 8–9.
FPG/ Michael Hart: 11 left; Andrea Sperling: 42; Colour Box: 46; Telegraph Colour Library: 74, 124–125; Ron Thomas: 76–77; Arthur Tilley: 99 left; Toyohiro Yamada: 106.
The Glasgow Museum: 114.
Anne Hamersky: 60.
Bob Hand: 66.
The Image Bank/ Maria Taglienti: 11 right; Steven Hunt: 40–41; Eric Meola: 45 bottom; Alberto Inrocci: 75; Ira Block: 78; Chris A. Wilton: 80–81; G&M David de Lossy: 85 top; Simon Wilkinson: 88–89; Frank Wise: 99 right.
Liaison International/ J&M Studios: 28;

James Schnepf: 35 top; Douglas Burrows: 35 bottom; Lien/Nebauer: 43 bottom; Larry Mayer: 58; Michael Renaudeau: 84–85.
Robert Llewellyn: 94.
Minden Pictures: 51.
Steve Moriarity: 104–105.
Nonstock/ Luca Zampredi: 102.
Richard Pasley: 44 top.
Picture Perfect/ Alex Sanders: 64–65 bottom.
Questar: 110.
H. Armstrong Roberts/ Camerique: 36.
Dana Sigall: 107.
Stock Market/ Tom Sanders: 27; Zefa/Mael: 44 center; Mugshots: 50.
Superstock: 13, 38, 72–73, 93.
Joan Ellen Thomas: 96–97.
Tony Stone Images: 30, 61, 108–109, 112–113, 113; Olaf Soot: 6; David Young Wolff: 11 top; David Hiser: 12; Patrick Ingrand: 16–17; John Lund: 24–25; Thomas Brase: 26; Wm. J. Hebert: 32–33; Chad Slattery: 43 top; Gary Yeowall: 48–49; World Perspective: 52; Glen Allison: 56–57; Bruce Ayres: 62; John Turner: 64–65 top; Mitch Kezar: 69; Theo Allofs: 82; David Higgs: 84 top; Barbara Filet: 84 bottom; Laurence Dutton: 85 bottom; Richard Passmore: 90; Darrell Gulin: 98–99.
Uniphoto: 21, 53.
Viesti Associates, Inc.: 14.
Bill Wittman: 20.

General Consultant
Rev. Joseph A. Komonchak, Ph.D.

Official Theological Consultant
Most Rev. Edward K. Braxton, Ph.D., S.T.D.
Auxiliary Bishop of St. Louis

Publisher
Gerard F. Baumbach, Ed.D.

Editor in Chief
Moya Gullage

Pastoral Consultant
Rev. Msgr. John F. Barry

Scriptural Consultant
Rev. Donald Senior, C.P., Ph.D., S.T.D.

General Editors
Norman F. Josaitis, S.T.D.
Rev. Michael J. Lanning, O.F.M.

Catechetical and Liturgical Consultants
Eleanor Ann Brownell, D. Min.
Joseph F. Sweeney
Helen Hemmer, I.H.M.
Mary Frances Hession
Maureen Sullivan, O.P., Ph.D.
Don Boyd

"The Ad Hoc Committee to Oversee the Use of the Catechism,
National Conference of Catholic Bishops,
has found this catechetical text to be in conformity
with the *Catechism of the Catholic Church*."

Nihil Obstat
✠ Most Reverend George O. Wirz
Censor Librorum

Imprimatur
✠ Most Reverend William H. Bullock
Bishop of Madison
July 21, 1997

The *Nihil Obstat* and *Imprimatur* are official
declarations that a book or pamphlet is free of
doctrinal or moral error. No implication is contained
therein that those who have granted the *Nihil Obstat*
and *Imprimatur* agree with the contents, opinions, or
statements expressed.

Printed in the United States of America.

S is a registered trademark of William H. Sadlier, Inc.

Home Office:
9 Pine Street
New York, NY 10005–1002

ISBN: 0-8215-5652-5
13 14 15 16 17 18 19 20 21 WEBC 14 13 12 11 10

A Course on Catholic Belief

Part I: Faith and Revelation

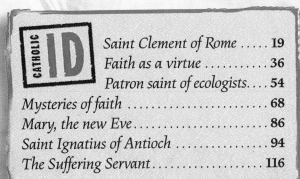

The Amazing Search for God

Introduction to Creed Part I

No matter where you go, you will always find the influence of religion. Whether you stay in your hometown or travel around the globe, you will always find it. In fact some of the world's most beautiful structures were built because of religion and the search for God. Why is this so? How would you explain it?

Our Catholic faith gives us the answer to these questions: "The desire for God is written in the human heart" because we were created by God and for God (*Catechism of the Catholic Church, 27*). What does this mean? It means that the search for God is a part of being human. And it has been that way from the beginning.

Did all people find the one true God in their search? Did everyone discover the truth about God? Let's take a look. As we do, we will begin to realize even more that being a Catholic is something very special.

Even before the dawn of history, primitive people were searching for God. When they looked far into the night sky and saw the moon and the stars, what did they think of those shining lights? When a baby was born or someone died, what thoughts raced through their minds? Where did the world around them come from? Who or what kept the stars in their places?

All the evidence that modern men and women have discovered points to the fact that most, if not all, ancient peoples had their own ideas of a god or gods and their own practice of a religion. It seems that some form of religious expression has been part of human experience from the beginning.

Today we know that the practice of religion is universal. It is found all over the world. If you look at any period of history, you will discover human beings engaged in religious activities. In fact we can say that of all the creatures on earth human beings are the only religious creatures and that religion has always been an important part of the human story.

The search for God has taken many different paths. Now we know why the Church teaches that the desire for God is written in the human heart. But how do we as Catholics fit into this search for God? Where are our roots, and why are we so different?

About three thousand years ago, a new religion, the religion of the Israelites, was born. It began with one individual who was invited by the one true God into a new relationship such as the world had never known. This individual was Abraham. No longer would he worship many gods. Now he knew that there was only one God. Abraham and his family risked everything to follow God's invitation. Abraham did not know where it would lead. All he knew was that this God, who was calling him, was like no other.

From this divine invitation and Abraham's response, there eventually emerged two of the world's great religions: Judaism and Christianity. What made these religions so special? What set them apart from all the other religions of the world? The answer to these questions can be found in one word: revelation.

So it is with revelation that we begin the study of our faith—of what we believe as Catholics. During the weeks ahead we will be challenged to discover in a new and deeper way the uniqueness and beauty of our Catholic faith. Let's set out on our amazing search for God.

A Divine and Awesome Invitation

No one knows the Father except the Son and anyone to whom the Son wishes to reveal him.

Matthew 11:27

HOW do you really get to know someone?
How do you let others know about yourself,
about what you are thinking and feeling?

Getting to Know Someone

It may sound strange, but we can live next door to
people and never really get to know them. Why is
this so? Perhaps they are shy or speak a different
language. Maybe they attend a different school or
place of worship. It could be that we have never
invited them to know us. Whatever the reason may
be, all we can say about these neighbors is what we
see or what others have told us about them. The
only way we can really know them is if they tell us
about themselves.

When people make themselves known to us and
tell us who they are, we say that they reveal
themselves to us. When this happens, we really
get to know them for the first time. Take, for
example, popular singers or sports figures we
admire. We listen to their music or perhaps watch
every game they play, but we may never know
anything about their personal lives or beliefs.
These will remain unknown to us unless we meet
the people we admire face-to-face or find out,
through TV or magazine interviews, what they
have to say about themselves.

Getting to Know God

Once we understand the way we get to know
someone, we are getting close to knowing the
meaning of revelation. Revelation is the act of a
person. It is the opening up of one person to
another. What does this have to do with God?
It is what God has done. God has opened himself
to us and has let us know his deepest Self.

Of course, even before any special act of revelation,
God had already left his "footprints" in creation.
Along with all other peoples, we see God's
footprints in the wonders of our universe. God is
like a great artist who can be recognized in his
work. But we cannot know God as he really is
unless he tells us more about himself, unless God
reveals himself to us.

10

You may wish to read part of Abraham's story in Genesis 12:1–8 and 15:1–7. What promise did God make to Abraham? Write it here or in your journal.

And that is exactly what God did. God began the process by revealing himself to Abraham. What God did was something completely new for the human race, something unheard of by any other people. In Abraham, God was choosing a people for his own, inviting them into a close relationship with him. These people were the ancient Israelites, the ancestors of the Jews and our ancestors in faith, too. This revealing God would be their God, and they would be his people. God would not remain unknown to them; rather, he would be closer to them than they could ever imagine. So great would God be that no mere image or idol could contain him.

Lord of heaven and earth…is he who gives to everyone life and breath and everything" (Acts 17:22–25).

What was Paul saying to the people? In many ways he was praising the people for recognizing the footprints of God in creation. But he was also pointing out that they were worshiping an "Unknown God." They did not as yet know the God of Abraham, the God who had revealed himself as Lord of heaven and earth.

The words of Saint Paul remind us why the religions of Jews and Christians are different from all others. We believe in the one God, who revealed himself to us in a special way. It all began with Abraham. That is why both Jews and Christians are the descendants of Abraham. As we shall see, however, for Catholics and other Christians, God's revealing activity reached its high point in Jesus Christ.

Divine Revelation

How many times have you heard someone say that God loves you? How do you know it's true? How do we know that Jesus is really the Son of God? How do we know that God is even involved in our world and our lives?

Saint Paul talked about this greatness of God two thousand years ago. One day when he arrived in the ancient city of Athens, Greece, he looked around and saw that the city was filled with images of pagan gods. So he said to the people:

"You Athenians, I see that in every respect you are very religious. For as I walked around looking carefully at your shrines, I even discovered an altar inscribed, 'To an Unknown God.' What therefore you unknowingly worship, I proclaim to you. The God who made the world and all that is in it, the

We know the answers to these questions because God told us. The most important things we know about God come from one source: God himself. God making himself known to us is called *divine revelation*. It is called *divine* because it is an activity of God; it is called *revelation* because it is God making himself known to us in a deep and intimate way. Understanding divine revelation is essential to our whole life of faith. In fact it is the basis of everything Christians believe, and it helps to identify who we are as Catholics.

Because revelation is so basic to Catholic life, we should know its four most important features: (1) It happens over a long time. (2) It happens in history. (3) It happens between God and people. (4) It happens in community. Let's take a closer look at each of these features of revelation.

Over a Long Time   God chose to reveal himself gradually, over a long period, much as we ourselves do at times. As human beings we open ourselves to others as we get to know them better. We let others know about us little by little. It may even take a lifetime to get to know someone well.

If this is true for us, how much more so for God. That is because the mystery of God is so deep. It could never be revealed to us all at once; otherwise we would be overwhelmed by the majesty of God. The process of God revealing himself, therefore, has taken a long time. It began in a special way with Abraham and continued until it reached its high point in Jesus Christ. The New Testament explains God's revelation this way: "In times past, God spoke in partial and various ways to our ancestors through the prophets; in these last days, he spoke to us through a son" (Hebrews 1:1–2).

In History   God's revealing of himself did not just happen over time; it also happened in history. The exodus of the Israelites from slavery in Egypt, for example, was a real event. In that historical event the Israelites realized that God was with them and was responsible for freeing them from the hopelessness and despair of slavery. God was not just an impersonal bystander; he was personally involved in their lives. God continued to involve himself in the lives of the Israelites and their descendants. Then the greatest moment of God's involvement in human history happened: Jesus

was born. In Jesus, God was not only involving himself in history; God became a part of our history.

Between God and People   God doesn't send us an encyclopedia or a CD-ROM to tell us about himself. God interacts with people; he has a relationship with them. That is how God reveals himself to people. Think of our ancestors in faith. God called Abraham, and Abraham and the people responded to God's call. God spoke to Moses at the burning bush. Moses and the people responded and entered into a covenant agreement with God. He would be their God; they would be his people. God spoke through the prophets and called the people to be true to the agreement they had made with God. Finally, God spoke to us in his Son and called us to discipleship.

We see, then, that revelation always happens between God and people. If we were to compare revelation with a conversation, it would not be a monologue, a one-sided conversation. It would be a dialogue with two sides: God on one side and us on the other.

Catholic Teachings

About Revelation

The Church knows just how important revelation is and how important it is for us to understand it clearly. That is why all the bishops of the world talked about revelation at the Second Vatican Council. At this greatest of Church gatherings in our time, the bishops made sure everyone would know how important revelation is by writing an entire document about it.

In Community God's revelation always takes place in a community setting. Even though God revealed himself to some individuals, such as Abraham and Moses, this revelation wasn't just for these individuals. God's revelation was for the whole community.

Is this community setting really important? It is very important! Human beings always depend on one another to get the "big picture" of things. Usually it takes the work of several people to clarify complicated issues. Think, for example, how many people have contributed to our scientific understanding of the universe. No one person could have done the job. Think, too, of family and friends, of how often they help us to understand others and the events of our lives. So it is with our understanding of God's revelation. It would take the whole community to experience fully God's revealing activity, and it would take many individuals to understand and interpret it.

Are you surprised that God has been so active in our lives? Why do you think God revealed himself gradually, over such a long period of time?

Imagine that you and a group of your friends were sent by Saint Paul to speak to the people of a great city like Athens. How would you prepare to speak to the people? What would you tell them about God's revelation to us?

Some people claim to have special messages from God, special "private" revelations. What should Catholics think about such things?

OnLine WITH THE PARISH

The Church teaches that the desire for God is in every human heart. Work with a liturgy-planning team in your parish and together make up some petitions for the Prayer of the Faithful. You might pray that people will show respect for all religions and that everyone will be brought to a greater knowledge and love of God.

YOU ARE MY WITNESSES

Things to Think About

Why is revelation at the very heart of our Catholic faith?

Do you believe that God is deeply involved in your life? Explain.

WORDS to REMEMBER

Find and define:

divine revelation

_____

_____

_____

_____

CHAPTER 2

DISCOVERING THE TRUTH

Your word is a lamp for my feet,
a light for my path.

Psalm 119:105

FAMILIES are great storytellers. They share and pass on stories of grandparents and great-grandparents who came from other lands to begin new lives. They tell of family "characters": Grandpa Charlie, who was in politics; Uncle Jack, who spent some time in jail; Great-Aunt Harriet, a suffragette who wrote novels on the side. There are usually family heroes, too, people who saved lives or raised their children against great odds. In some families there might even be a saint or two.

Does your family tell and pass on its stories? How? Aside from being interesting or funny, why do you think family stories are important?

The handing on of revelation was described beautifully by Clement of Rome. He was a bishop of Rome and the earliest Christian writer outside the New Testament. Writing around A.D. 95, Clement said, "The apostles received the gospel for us from the Lord Jesus Christ; and Jesus Christ was sent forth from God. Christ, in other words, comes with a message from God, and the apostles with a message from Christ."

From Generation to Generation

God not only revealed himself but made sure that his revelation would be passed on from generation to generation. How did this happen?

The Old Testament In ancient Israel the story of God's revelation was handed on to the next generation by word of mouth. People talked, sang, and told their stories about the living experience of their community with God and all that God did for them. This handing on of their unwritten traditions by word of mouth is known as oral tradition. Later some of this oral tradition of the Israelites was written down under the guidance of the Holy Spirit. This written record of divine revelation came to be known as the Old Testament.

The Fullness of Revelation Remember that God's revelation took place in the history of the community. It took place over a long period of time and reached its high point in Jesus Christ. That is why we say that what was recorded in the Old Testament was brought to completion in Christ our Lord. In him the fullness of God's revelation was made to us because God was speaking through his Son. For this reason Jesus was truly the Word of God. In Jesus, God spoke to us his fullest and final word. There will never be another. That is because Jesus brought the fullness of God's revelation to the world.

The New Testament Filled with excitement about their experience of Jesus, the apostles and the first followers of Jesus wanted to share the good news. They wanted everyone to know what Jesus had taught them, why he came, and what he did for the world. This good news of Jesus was first handed on by the apostles and the early Church by word of mouth. Later some of this oral tradition was also put into writing under the guidance of the Holy Spirit. This written record of divine revelation came to be known as the New Testament.

The New Testament is the most important written record that comes to us from the time of the apostles and the early Church. Because it is a written document, it is permanent and cannot be changed. Neither can the Old Testament. Both are inspired by God. Catholics have a deep respect for both the Old and the New Testaments. Together they are known as Sacred Scripture.

Write one way you can show reverence and respect for Sacred Scripture.

In the New Testament the short Letter of Jude, which is only twenty-five verses long, was written to warn the early Christians against false teachers. They were reminded that the teachings of the Church came from the preaching of the apostles, who were guided by the Holy Spirit. The community was to persevere in "the faith that was once for all handed down…" (Jude 3).

Is Scripture Alone Enough?

The answer to this question is no. Scripture can never stand alone. It needs tradition, the living experience of the community, to make it come alive. In fact, as we have seen, Scripture comes from the living tradition of the community. This living tradition existed before Scripture was written down and helped to form it.

Does Scripture give a complete picture of Jesus, the early Church, and all that God has revealed? No written record can do that. Even at the end of John's Gospel, for example, we read, "There are also many other things that Jesus did, but if these were to be described individually, I do not think the whole world would contain the books that would be written" (John 21:25). In a dramatic way John was telling us that no written record can completely capture a living experience.

Even though the New Testament may not give a complete picture of Jesus, it nevertheless gives a truthful and permanent picture. For example, the New Testament records the fact that Jesus died on the cross and rose from the dead. This truth cannot be denied or changed. The written word of Scripture gives us a constant guideline for our beliefs. The Church can never abandon, ignore, or change this written record.

It is also the responsibility of the Church to teach the true meaning of Scripture—that is, to interpret it—in every age. No type of written record can pass from generation to generation without being interpreted. That is why Scripture is truly a book of the Church.

It is clear, then, that the handing on of God's revelation comes to us through tradition and Scripture. These two are so closely related to each other that we cannot understand one without the other.

 Tell one thing about Jesus that you have learned from the Scriptures.

20

A Great Treasure

The apostles and the early Church community realized that they had a great treasure to share with the whole world. And what was this treasure? The truths of revelation! Today Catholics call this treasure the deposit of faith. The *deposit of faith* includes all the truths entrusted, or handed over, by Christ to the apostles and the early Church. These truths, contained in tradition and Scripture, are now handed on by the Church as a treasure to the world.

Why do we call this treasure a *deposit*? The reason goes back to biblical times. Then a deposit was thought of as something special. It was so special, in fact, that a deposit was entrusted to someone to guard. That is why Saint Paul wrote to his companion Timothy and instructed him to hand on the whole message of revelation and to protect it from what was false. Paul wrote, "Guard what has been entrusted to you" (1 Timothy 6:20). Later he wrote to Timothy, "Guard this rich trust with the help of the holy Spirit…" (2 Timothy 1:14).

Paul must have thought that the deposit of faith was very important. That is why he used the words "rich trust" to describe it. The deposit of faith is important for us, too. It is that treasure entrusted to the Church by Christ until the end of time. It is a rich trust for us because it is about God's revelation, which lies at the very heart of our Catholic faith.

Have you ever thought of your faith as a "rich trust"? How can you both "guard what has been entrusted to you" and share it with others?

A Dynamic Treasure

As we have already said, the deposit of faith includes everything that God entrusted to the Church community in Scripture and tradition. Remember that Scripture means Old Testament and New Testament. Both were inspired by the Holy Spirit. But what is tradition? *Tradition* is the whole dynamic life and activity of the Church.

21

A Living Treasure

Being a deposit does not mean that the teachings of revelation are like a buried treasure or a museum piece to be preserved and dusted off from time to time. Rather the deposit of faith is a living thing, a dynamic treasure meant to be proclaimed and lived in each age. The Church guards this treasure by making it meaningful to all people throughout the world.

Will there be any further or new revelations from God to the community? No. The Church teaches that the fullness of God's revelation has come to us in Jesus Christ. God has told us in Jesus everything that we need to hear for every age. The community of the Church can never accept anything that would claim to go beyond Christ. Furthermore, any type of so-called private revelation—even if it is recognized by the Church—does not belong to the deposit of faith. Whatever God may have communicated since apostolic times to privileged individuals—for their own good or the good of the Church in a particular age—can add nothing to the deposit of faith.

Take a look at the chart to see what tradition includes and why it is so dynamic.

Write one way that you have participated in the tradition of the Church.

The Church's Dynamic Life: Tradition's Many Parts

Part	Description	Example
Teachings, customs, practices handed down from the time of the apostles	The handing on of the Church's dynamic life and beliefs either by word of mouth or in writing, but not necessarily found in Scripture	The practice of baptizing infants that has come down to us from the Church's earliest days
Creeds	Official statements of belief	Nicene Creed
Teachings of Church councils	Teachings from important gatherings of the world's bishops with the pope	Second Vatican Council (1962–1965)
Teachings from the Church Fathers	Writings from saintly scholars of the first eight centuries of the Church who helped to explain and hand on the Christian message	Clement of Rome, bishop of Rome around A.D. 95
The Church's worship and liturgy	The whole life and experience of the Church as it gathers together to worship God and hear God's word	God making himself known to us today as Scripture is proclaimed and preached at Mass

How did God make sure that his revelation would be passed on to us?

Why must we guard the deposit of faith as a "rich trust"?

In the fourth century Saint Jerome complained to a friend about the sloppy way in which some Christians proclaimed the word of God. To read Scripture aloud without preparation was "circus stuff," he said. He meant that this was showing disrespect for God's word. Invite whoever trains lectors in your parish to talk with your group about this ministry. Explore the ways both lectors and listeners can treasure the word of God.

YOU ARE MY WITNESSES

Things to Think About

What does it mean to you when we say that we are a people of tradition, that for Catholics the past is a living treasure and counts a great deal?

Sometimes we meet people who say that the answers to all life's questions can be found in the Bible. As a thoughtful Catholic would you agree or disagree with that statement? Why?

WORDS to REMEMBER

Find and define:

deposit of faith

_____

_____

_____

_____

23

CHAPTER 3

DIVINE GIFT AND HUMAN RESPONSE

We walk by faith, not by sight.

2 Corinthians 5:7

ONE of the natural wonders of Yellowstone National Park in Wyoming is Old Faithful. This geyser shoots thousands of gallons of hot water and steam high into the air each time it spouts. Early explorers named it Old Faithful because it seemed to erupt "faithfully" every sixty-five or seventy minutes.

Further observation indicated that the eruptions of the geyser occur more irregularly than first thought. Nevertheless millions of tourists gather at the geyser each year, hoping to see the fountainlike column of water burst into the sky. They "believe" that Old Faithful will put on its spectacular performance once again for them.

What do the words "faithful," "believe," and "faith" mean to you? In terms of religion would you describe yourself as a faithful person? Are you a believer? What does faith mean to you?

Seeking the Truth

People express what is true or false for them in many ways. Some say, "I *think* that this is true, not that." Others say, "I *believe* that this is true, not that." Still others might say, "I *know* that this is true, not that." Do all these expressions mean the same thing? Or does our choice of words make a difference?

If we say that we *think* something is true, we are expressing our opinion about something. For example, a farmer may say, "I think that I will have a very big harvest this year. My crops will grow well because of abundant rainfall, no floods, and plenty of good weather." The farmer is expressing an opinion about the future and is fairly certain that this thought will come true.

If we say that we *know* something is true, it means that we are absolutely certain that something will happen. We base our knowledge on concrete facts. For example, scientists have developed vaccines against terrible diseases such as polio, measles, and mumps. Over many years of experimentation and testing, they had visible proof and knew that the vaccines would work to save many lives. We know that the vaccines work today.

If we say that we *believe* in or *have faith* in something or someone, we are putting our trust in our past experiences or in someone else. Belief is generally the result of putting our trust in another person. For example, you hear a rumor that your best friend has been caught shoplifting. He or she tells you that this is a lie. You believe your friend because in the past he or she has always been truthful and reliable. You trust your friend and believe in his or her innocence.

It may sound strange to some people, but much of what we know comes through faith. Think about this: Have you ever been to Antarctica? Most of us have not, but we believe that Antarctica exists. Others have been there and have told us about it. We have seen pictures and videos. We can point to it on a map. It is reasonable to accept the fact that Antarctica exists. It would be unreasonable for us to deny its reality and to say that Antarctica was dreamed up on a Hollywood set or designed from a computer model. People would think that we were crazy. So although we have never been to Antarctica ourselves, we believe, on the basis of the experience of others, that it does exist.

In many ways, then, to live is to believe. To be a person of belief does not mean that we live in a fantasy world or a world filled with doubts. Our beliefs are certain because they are reasonable. Nevertheless belief, or faith, includes a risk. We may, for example, put our trust in the wrong person or make a wrong judgment about our experience. But we take these risks every day. We place our trust in people day in and day out. We accept the existence of things that we cannot see or touch ourselves.

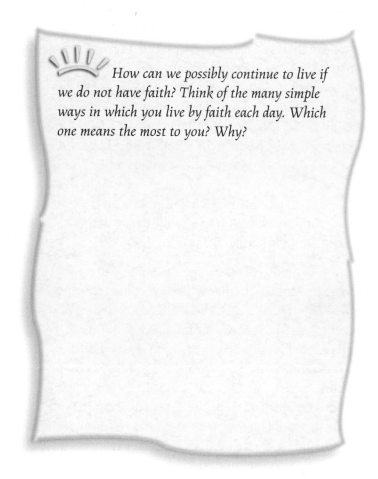

How can we possibly continue to live if we do not have faith? Think of the many simple ways in which you live by faith each day. Which one means the most to you? Why?

Religious Faith

Each day when we awaken, we share an unspoken faith that the sun will rise and set, that the pull of gravity will keep us firmly planted on earth, and that the atmosphere will be good enough for us to breathe. We also have faith in people, especially members of our family, our friends, and those in whom we place our trust. We call this type of faith natural faith, since it has to do with our everyday experience of the natural world.

There is, however, another type of faith. This kind of faith is religious faith. It is the basis for our personal relationship with God. Religious faith is not only faith in something; it is faith in Someone. It is faith in God.

To understand this kind of faith, we can turn to Abraham. In the Old Testament he is presented as the model of faith. Remember the story of Abraham told in Genesis 12—22. God promised to make him the father of many nations despite the fact that Abraham and Sarah, his wife, were both beyond the normal age for becoming parents. Later Abraham was called to offer his only son, Isaac, as a sacrifice to God. Even though Abraham's heart was broken

at the thought of losing Isaac, Abraham's faith never wavered. He was ready to risk everything for God.

God rewarded Abraham's faith by sparing Isaac's life. The faith of Abraham had been tested by God. God showed that he was true to the agreement he had made with Abraham: All the nations of the earth would share in God's blessing through Isaac because of Abraham's faith.

In the Bible the word *faith* means "to hold firm to." Faith in God is a holding on to God; we anchor our lives on his word. We can do this because God alone is worthy of our complete trust. God alone is our strength. Jesus reminded us of this when he said that all things are possible for those who believe. Faith is so important that even a small amount of faith can "move" mountains (Matthew cf. 17:20).

 Describe a time when you felt that you could move mountains.

A Gift from God

How do we get faith? Do we arrive at faith on our own? To answer these questions, we must get to the heart of what faith really is. And that is God's grace.

Grace is a gift from God and a participation in the very life of God. The grace of faith enables us to begin to know God as God knows himself. That is why faith is a virtue; it is a power. Faith gives us the power to go beyond our human understanding and beyond what we can see and feel and touch around us. We cannot do this on our own. Faith empowers us to see through the "eyes of God." This means that faith is a supernatural gift from God; it is a gift that goes beyond our natural powers. As Saint Paul says, "We walk by faith, not by sight" (2 Corinthians 5:7).

29

Does this mean that without God's grace we cannot have faith? Are we incapable on our own of believing all that God has revealed? Yes, that is exactly what we are saying! God's grace and our free cooperation with it are essential to faith.

Without grace our human powers alone cannot enable us to be people of faith. The reason for this is that by faith we know God and God's revelation through the knowledge God has of himself. This sort of knowledge obviously goes beyond our natural powers. This is why Saint Paul could say, "For by grace you have been saved through faith, and this is not from you; it is the gift of God" (Ephesians 2:8).

We can say, then, that *faith* is a supernatural gift from God. It enables us to open ourselves to God and to accept all that God has revealed. When we have faith, we know God through the knowledge God has of himself. In this sense faith is actually the beginning of eternal life, in which we shall know God "face to face."

People who do not have faith do not know what they are missing. What do you as a person of faith think that they are missing?

What is the difference between knowing and believing?

Is it possible to have faith without God's grace?

YOU ARE MY WITNESSES

Every year the parish helps prepare people who wish to become Catholics. These people are called *catechumens*, and the steps they take toward membership in the Church are called the *Rite of Christian Initiation* (RCIA). Members of the parish help in this process by becoming sponsors of the catechumens. Find out about the RCIA in your parish. Pray for those preparing to proclaim their faith in Jesus Christ and become members of the Catholic Church.

Things to Think About

A wise man has said that to be a believer means to take a "leap of faith."

What do you think that means?

What does the believer leave behind?

What does the believer leap toward?

Should we consider people who do not believe in God to be bad people? Why or why not?

WORDS to REMEMBER

Find and define:

faith

_____

_____

_____

_____

31

CHAPTER

A LIFELONG
CHALLENGE

Be on your guard, stand firm in the faith, be courageous, be strong.

1 Corinthians 16:13

THERE is a story about a rabbi who prayed, "Lord, make me like Abraham! I'll set out in faith; I'll answer your call, but first, make me like Abraham."

God answered him, saying, "Look, I've already got an Abraham!"

What does God's "answer" to the rabbi mean? What does Abraham's story tell you about faith? What does faith mean to you?

Describing Faith

Faith comes from "what is heard." It is not like the study of history, which comes from digging up facts and researching past events. Faith depends, not on our brilliance or position in the world, but on what we hear and on what we accept. In Scripture we read:

> For "everyone who calls on the name of the Lord will be saved." But how can they call on him in whom they have not believed? And how can they believe in him of whom they have not heard? And how can they hear without someone to preach? And how can people preach unless they are sent?. . .Thus faith comes from what is heard, and what is heard comes through the word of Christ.
> Romans 10:13–17

Does this mean that faith is blind, that we accept anything, even if it is totally unreasonable? In no way! Faith has some definite characteristics, or qualities.

Reasonable   The first quality of faith is that it is reasonable; it is not blind. God has made human beings intelligent creatures. God wants us to understand as much as we can about our faith; this means that we have to ask questions. Faith always seeks understanding.

The power of human reason, our ability to think things out, should never be in conflict with faith. That is because God is the source of both faith and reason. The more we use our reason and intelligence to investigate the world, the more we see God's creative hand at work. God cannot contradict the truth of what he has created. For example, God cannot make a square circle because the nature of a square and that of a circle are directly opposed to each other.

Faith does not take the place of reason, personal experience, human searching, or learning from others. Faith builds on our human abilities and works through them.

Certain The second quality of faith is that it is certain. This is because faith rests on God's word and God cannot lie. As we read in Scripture, "If we accept human testimony, the testimony of God is surely greater" (1 John 5:9).

Does this mean that all the truths of our faith will be perfectly clear to us or that we will somehow remove the mystery of faith? No. It simply means that we may not grasp or understand everything right away or completely.

The funny thing about human beings is that we would like everything to be simple, without any complications. But real life is not like that; it is complex. If we look in a mathematics book, for example, we are going to find that some ideas are difficult to grasp at first. But we shouldn't be afraid of the challenge of new ideas. The same can be said of science, technology, history, or geography. Why should people expect anything different when it comes to the truths of faith? We do not have to be geniuses to accept our faith, but we do have to work hard to understand it according to our abilities. Faith is more than just a feeling.

What are some of the questions you have in seeking to understand your faith?

Communal The third quality of faith is that it is communal. When we respond in faith to God's revelation, we do so as individuals, but not in isolation from others. Faith happens in a community. This is the way God deals with humankind—through a community. We receive faith through the Church, just as we receive life through our parents. We did not give ourselves faith, just as we did not give ourselves life. Faith, therefore, is not simply a personal, solitary act.

Free The fourth quality of faith is that it is free. When we place our faith and trust in God, we do so freely; God does not force us to believe against our will. If this were not so, faith would be against our human dignity as created by God.

Professed The fifth quality of faith is that it must be professed. By this we mean that faith is not just held inside us; it must also be expressed by our actions and by our words. This means that we must give witness to our faith. It is not just something that we think about. Faith that is not lived and professed is, in fact, unbelief.

What do you find most challenging in living and giving witness to your faith? Write your thoughts in your journal.

A Priceless Gift

Some people feel that their religious education, the exploration of their faith, ends in the eighth grade or after celebrating the sacraments of initiation: Baptism, Confirmation, and Eucharist. They feel that after these celebrations there is nothing left to learn. But such an idea could not be further from the truth. Exploring our faith is a lifetime project.

Our faith is a priceless gift, but it can lose its luster or even be lost altogether. How can we make sure this does not happen? We do this first of all by taking the time to learn about our faith. This involves more than just memorizing facts or names or dates. It means exploring our faith so deeply that it will make a real difference in our lives. After all, how can we really appreciate something unless we know more about it?

CATHOLIC ID You may notice that Catholics use the word *faith* in two different ways. We might say, "That person is a person of faith." This use of the word refers to faith as a virtue, as the grace of faith. We might also say, "I live by my Catholic faith." This use of the word refers to what we believe, or the content of faith.

How do you think a young person can grow in faith? What will you do to become a more faithful person? Write your thoughts here or in your journal.

Besides learning about our faith, we must also nourish it by the way we live our lives. We do this through the life-giving relationship we have with God in prayer. At the center of our prayer life are the Eucharist and the other sacraments. We also grow in faith when we actively participate in the life of the Church. Faith never stands alone but is lived by a community of people.

What happens if we do not explore our faith, or nourish it in prayer, or participate in the faith life of the community? Our faith will grow weak. Then, one day, there may be nothing left of it to hold on to. We would have wasted God's precious gift to us. But this will not happen if we take up the lifelong challenge of growing in faith.

Living Without Faith

Generally speaking there are two kinds of people who seem to live their lives without faith. They are called atheists and agnostics.

Atheists *Atheists* are people who deny the existence of God and who, therefore, live their lives without God. Although we may not know any individuals who claim to be atheists, many people seem to live as if they were atheists. This includes people who never think about God. It also includes people who speak highly about faith and religion but leave it at that level, the level of talking. Actions speak louder than words, however. Catholics who loudly proclaim that they are members of the Church but never practice their faith are, in fact, living an atheistic lifestyle.

Are atheists by definition bad people? Of course not! Some people practice no formal religion and are convinced that God does not exist. But many of them care very deeply about living a life full of values, including care for others, care for the earth, and striving for peace.

Why, then, are they atheists? There are many possible reasons. One may be that no one has ever approached them to bring them the good news of the gospel. Another reason may be that these nonbelievers spoke with believers who did not seem to have intelligent explanations about what they believe. Perhaps the nonbelievers met people who claimed to be religious but gave poor example, turning them off to God. Another reason may be that they rejected the gift of faith that God offered to them. Whatever the reason, we can never judge others, since we do not know their circumstances.

Agnostics *Agnostics* are people who cannot decide whether or not to believe in God. They say that God's existence or the answers to life's most important questions are unknowable at best and are even unprovable. They seem to put their trust only in those things that can be seen or felt or heard or touched or experienced in a physical way.

Knowing how wonderful faith is, we can say that people without faith do not know what they are missing. That is because faith is participation in the very life of God and the knowledge God has of himself. Does this mean that we as people of faith can never have moments of doubt in our lives? No. We would not be human if we did not have some doubts. But as believers we can always turn to Jesus. Remember, it was Jesus who said, "Do not let your hearts be troubled. You have faith in God; have faith also in me" (John 14:1).

 What advice would you give to someone who seems to be having problems with faith?

Scripture UPDATE

There are many places in the gospels in which Jesus speaks about faith. One time he was talking about the gift of faith and said, "No one can come to me unless the Father who sent me draw him" (John 6:44). Another time Jesus was talking about faith to the apostle Thomas, who had doubted Jesus' resurrection and would only be satisfied with visible proof. Jesus said, "Blessed are those who have not seen and have believed" (John 20:29). What do these words of Jesus say to you?

Suppose you met someone who said to you, "People of faith never have any doubts." How would you respond to that person?

What do we mean when we say that faith must be professed?

God has called us to be members of a faith community. Alone we are like twigs, easily broken. Together we are like redwoods, whose strength and beauty inspire confidence and awe. Young people especially need to experience themselves as vital members of the parish community. Consider the ways in which your group can help young people to feel more at home in the parish. Plan a project to reach out to those who seem to be outside of parish life.

YOU ARE MY WITNESSES

How would you respond to the following statement: No one can tell me what to believe. Faith is only a personal matter.

What do you find challenging about being a believer?

Find and define:

atheists

_____

_____

_____

_____

THE GOD WHO REVEALS

CHAPTER 5

Glory to God in the highest.

Luke 2:14

HOW do we know that God exists?
Can we prove God's existence?

Arguing for God

Ever since people began to think about the origin of the world and the meaning of life, they have wondered whether or not God exists.

The greatest thinkers of humanity have struggled with this question. Some of them have tried to prove that God exists. Of course they were not thinking of proof in the scientific sense of the word. God and the life of faith cannot be analyzed in a test tube. God's existence cannot be proved in a laboratory.

What these great thinkers did come up with were a number of convincing arguments for the existence of God. These arguments point to God and offer a reasonable basis for faith. We will look at three of the arguments.

The First Cause   One argument for the existence of God can be called the "nothing is caused by itself" argument. It begins with the idea that everything must have a cause, an explanation for its origin. When we see a beautifully carved statue, for example, the first question we ask is, "Who was the artist?" We know that such a fine work of art was not simply found in a quarry as a finished piece. It took time and talent for a sculptor to carve it and make it a work of art.

The same can be said of the universe. We look around and ask, "Where did this marvel come from? What caused the universe and our solar system?" An immediate answer might be that it evolved to its present state over billions of years.

But then the next question must be, "What caused evolution in the first place?" We can continue with a thousand questions and answers, but at the end the same question can be asked: "What caused that?" When we finally arrive at a first cause, we reach the end of the line. Beyond this First Cause we can go no further. And that First Cause is God! Nobody caused God to be. Nobody made God.

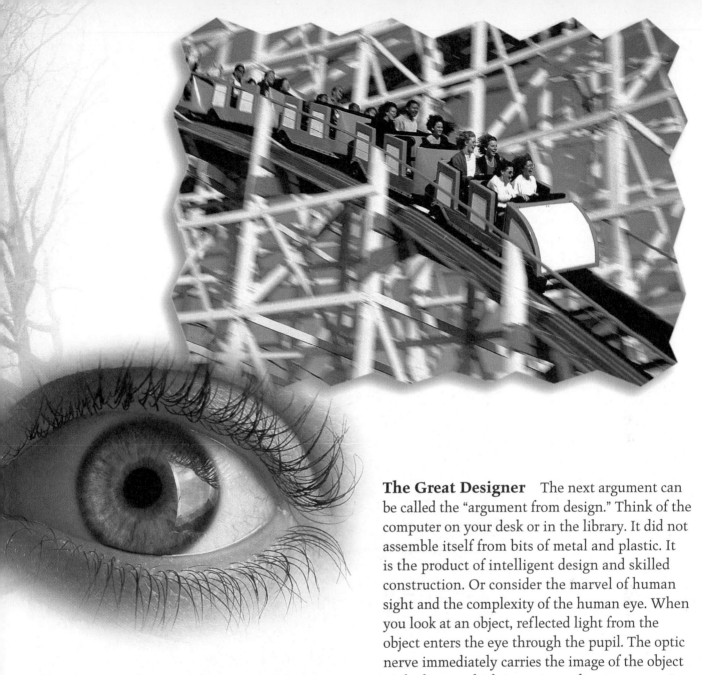

The Great Designer   The next argument can be called the "argument from design." Think of the computer on your desk or in the library. It did not assemble itself from bits of metal and plastic. It is the product of intelligent design and skilled construction. Or consider the marvel of human sight and the complexity of the human eye. When you look at an object, reflected light from the object enters the eye through the pupil. The optic nerve immediately carries the image of the object to the brain, which interprets what you are seeing. What a masterpiece the eye is! Do you think this wonderful organ came about by chance? Or was there an intelligent cause behind it?

What can be said about a computer or an eye also applies to the universe. It, too, is a complex and magnificent masterpiece. The argument from design suggests that the universe did not happen by chance but had an intelligent designer. This Great Designer is God.

Think of another marvel of creation. In what way is it an argument for the existence of God?

Suppose scientists eventually were to discover that everything in creation came from one tiny cell. They announce, "This is the source of all creation." What question would still have to be asked about that cell?

The Unmoved Mover Another famous argument for the existence of God is based on movement and change. It is called the "unmoved mover" argument. From your study of science, you know that all things are in motion. Look at an atom, for example, and you will see moving electrons. The whole universe, in fact, is in motion and is evolving. Movement, of course, begins when something is moved by something else. But where did all this movement start? When we go back as far as we can go, we arrive at the point of a first mover. This Unmoved Mover is God.

These are some of the arguments for God's existence that have been proposed by the greatest thinkers of humanity. They are not proofs in the scientific sense, but they do make us think. They are reasonable ways to God; they are argued invitations to faith.

If you were going to give an argument for God's existence, what would it be?

God and Reason

Reason, the power we have to figure things out, can go a long way in helping us to understand who God is. When we look at the world around us, we see beauty, harmony, and order. Reasonable people say that someone must have designed the world with these things in mind.

What do we find in Scripture about God and reason? In Wisdom 13:1–9 we read that people can come to the knowledge of the one true God through the beauty and goodness seen in creation. After all, it makes sense to say that the author of the universe must be far superior and more wonderful than the world we see.

Saint Paul made this point in his New Testament letter to the Romans. Paul was very clear. He scolded those who refused to be reasonable and who turned to the worship of idols instead of God. Paul said:

For what can be known about God is evident to them, because God made it evident to them. Ever since the creation of the world, his invisible attributes of eternal power and divinity have been able to be understood and perceived in what he has made. As a result, they have no excuse; for although they knew God they did not accord him glory as God or give him thanks.
Romans 1:19–21

Perhaps Saint Paul was reminded of the famous line, "Fools say in their hearts, 'There is no God'" (Psalm 14:1).

Can human reason provide all the answers we need? No. Reason can take us only so far in our search for God. It cannot tell us much beyond the fact that a personal and caring God fashioned the world. For everything else we depend upon God to tell us about himself. We already know this from our study of revelation and faith. Divine revelation is the basis of our knowledge about God and our faith in God.

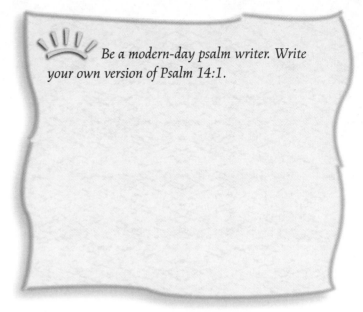

Be a modern-day psalm writer. Write your own version of Psalm 14:1.

God and Revelation

One truth that is basic to our Jewish-Christian heritage is that God is a personal God. God can never be reduced to being just a force of nature or a nameless power in the universe. Nor is God a lifeless image or idol to be worshiped. Our God is alive, and from the Old Testament we even learn God's name.

In ancient times the name of a person or thing was far more important than it is for us today. For the biblical writers, to know someone's name was to know that person. To have no name was to have no existence at all. In fact, to give a name was a powerful act. It was to give someone or something an identity. That is one reason God is described in Genesis as naming everything he created.

Have you ever pictured God whistling? The biblical writers did. They described God in wonderfully human terms. In the *New American Bible* translation, we read in Zechariah 10:8 that God whistles to gather his people together.

What else do we find out about God in the Old Testament? Yahweh is described as the living God. The writers of the Old Testament wanted it perfectly understood that God was not a lifeless idol of wood or stone but truly a living being. They even described God in human terms. In their descriptions Yahweh has a face with eyes, ears, mouth, and nostrils. He has hands and feet. He speaks, hears, smells, laughs, whistles, and walks. He feels joy, anger, hatred, love, disgust, and compassion. We know, of course, that God is not a human being with hands and feet. The biblical writers used these images to make their message clear: The living God communicates to his people and is thoroughly involved in their lives.

Now we can see why it was important to know God's name in Old Testament times. By revealing his name, God was identifying himself to us. Do you remember the story of Moses at the burning bush? It was from there that God sent Moses to the people. When Moses asked what he should tell his people about the God of their ancestors, God revealed to Moses the divine name. God said that his name was *Yahweh*, which means "I am who am" (Exodus 3:14).

God had a name! Yahweh was like no other name. Moses was to say to God's people, "I AM sent me to you" (Exodus 3:14). God's name showed the people that he was like no other god that could be imagined. Yahweh was the God who would personally save the people from slavery and make with them an everlasting covenant.

Our God is a personal God. What does that mean to you? Write your response here or in your journal.

Things to SHARE

Suppose that you tell your best friend that you want to be a scientist. Your friend says that no one can be a good Catholic and a good scientist at the same time. Share your responses to your friend with the group.

Your topic for an upcoming speech to young people is "Get with It: Believe in God!" Outline your talk, highlighting the main points.

OnLine WITH THE PARISH

If there are some "craft-y" people in your group, why not design a creation banner for your parish church. Here are some ideas to build on:

Let there be light.

Glory to God!

I AM who am.

The God who reveals.

Offer your banner to your pastor for display in church.

YOU ARE MY WITNESSES

Things to Think About

What is reasonable about belief in God? How does creation "speak" to us of God?

A nonbeliever asks you why someone "as intelligent as you" still believes in God. Your answer?

Words to Remember

Find and define:

Yahweh

_____

_____

_____

_____

THE GOD
WHO CREATES

The heavens declare the glory of God;
the sky proclaims its builder's craft.

Psalm 19:2

FOR thousands of years humanity's view of creation was limited to what could be seen by the unaided human eye. Then the telescope and the microscope were invented—and what wonders human beings have seen!

Some people are threatened by scientific advances, fearing that they will lead people to question or disbelieve in the existence of God. Others rejoice in the expanding horizons of science, finding in these new visions of the universe even more reasons to believe in the creator, the Great Designer, the First Cause.

What about you? Does science challenge your faith? strengthen your faith? Why?

God the Creator

God is the creator of all things. God created by his word; he spoke and everything came into being. That is the truth of faith we learn from the first page of the Bible. Creation is the creator's first word to us.

For many centuries people believed that all the statements in the Bible should be taken literally—exactly, word for word. That is why they thought that the universe was created literally in seven days as described in Genesis and that this took place about four thousand years before Christ. Some people still believe this.

In contrast modern science estimates that our universe is billions of years old. Scientists have different ideas of explaining how the universe began and how it evolved. Some think that a "big bang," or cosmic explosion of matter, eventually produced the whole universe. What should Catholics think? Should we be afraid of science?

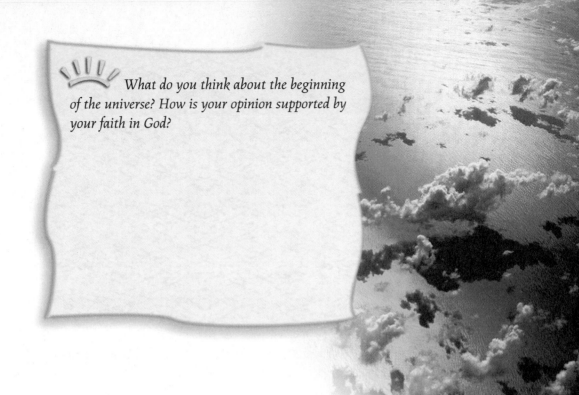

What do you think about the beginning of the universe? How is your opinion supported by your faith in God?

Interpreting the Creation Story

The inspired writers of Genesis were not interested in giving a scientific treatment of creation. Rather they wanted to tell the truths of faith. They also wanted to make clear the difference between their beliefs and those of their Mesopotamian neighbors, who followed pagan religions with many gods.

To understand the message of Genesis correctly, we must understand what the inspired authors had in mind when they were writing this book. Far from a scientific approach, these writers used the language of poetry to get their message across, telling the truth in "symbolic" and "figurative" language (*Catechism*, 362, 390). They wanted to point to truths that were unique to their understanding of God, that were not shared by other peoples.

In the Mesopotamian creation accounts, pagan gods had beginnings like mortal human beings. The biblical writers rejected this idea. They stressed that in the beginning God created the heavens and earth and everything in them. By doing so they were teaching that in the beginning there was nothing but God; then God created. God always was. He had no beginning.

The Genesis writers taught that there was only one God, the creator of everything. Unlike the pagan gods, the God of Israel existed before everything else. He was the *creator*: He created everything from nothing. God spoke, and by his word all things came into being.

How could the biblical writers best share their ideas with others? They told a story that pictured God as a worker who labored for six days of the week and rested on the seventh day—just as the people of Israel did. Thus, the biblical authors imagined God doing what a human worker might do. The first thing needed in a workshop would be light. So on the first day God created light. It did not matter to the writers that in their story the sun, moon, and stars would not be created until the fourth day.

The real message of Genesis, then, is about faith. It was never meant to deal with modern, scientific questions, but it is not opposed to science either. The Genesis account tells us *that* God created, not *how* God created. This is essential for Catholics to know and understand.

Can a message be communicated just as truly in poetry or story or song as in scientific language? Wouldn't the message "I love you" be difficult to say scientifically?

Faith and Science

Using telescopes, scientists peer into the vast reaches of space, hoping to unravel the mystery of the universe. Such scientific investigations have led to many theories. Through them we have come to see that the universe and all life evolved over billions of years. The inspired writers of Genesis, however, were not familiar with the theory of evolution. They were interested in teaching only one idea: Everything was made by God. This was the truth they wanted to share.

Today we know that science and religion are different. But they are not enemies; they both seek the truth. The Church welcomes the findings of science. To know more about the scientific details of creation is to know more about God the creator. However, such scientific knowledge will never replace the truth of Genesis—that God created the whole universe.

Most people wonder about God's existence at one time or another. The important thing is that this questioning can be a time of growth and change—if we are willing to do the hard work and take the time to understand who God is. What can you do to deepen this understanding?

CATHOLIC TEACHINGS

About God the Creator

The Church teaches us that God did not create the world and then leave it alone. God's work did not end with the act of creation. The whole universe continues to exist because God keeps it in existence. God's work of creation continues.

Attributes of God

Besides the word *creator*, there are other words that we use to describe God alone. These are God's attributes, or characteristics. The attributes of God, the supreme Being, include eternal, almighty, all-knowing, and all-present.

Eternal   Think about the time it would take to travel to galaxies that are millions of light-years away from us. For God these millions of years would be like an "instant." This is because God is eternal: He always was and always will be.

It may be hard for us to understand, but God is not subject to time as we are. Time is a measurable period that has a before and an after. But God is without beginning or end. God lives in eternity and has no need for time. Time is part of creation, but God is not part of creation. God is above it; God is timeless.

Material things change and pass away; God remains and is changeless. Creatures are subject to change because they are subject to time. Therefore they are finite; they have an end. God is infinite; he has no end. He is not limited by time.

Almighty   When we say that God is almighty, we mean that God can do all things. Another word for almighty is *omnipotent*. Who but the almighty God could create the universe and keep it in existence?

When we say that God is almighty, do we mean that he can do anything, even the impossible? Not at all. Just as God cannot make a square circle, since this would be a contradiction, it is impossible for God to commit a sin. That would make God imperfect and exactly like his creatures. God is perfect and could never do anything that goes against his perfection.

Can the almighty God work miracles? The answer is yes. Miracles are wonderful events that cannot be fully explained by the laws of nature. Miracles are done only by God for a purpose and show forth God's care and power.

The Church does not discourage people from praying for miracles, but it remains cautious about miracles in general. Whenever someone claims that a miracle has taken place, the Church first looks for a natural cause to explain it. Then, after a thorough investigation, only the Church declares whether or not a true miracle has occurred.

All-Knowing
Because God is eternal, he knows everything past, present, and future. Another word for all-knowing is *omniscient*. Does the fact that God is all-knowing mean that human beings are like puppets on a string? that we have no freedom? The answer is no.

An example may give us a rough idea of the way the all-knowing God interacts with us. Suppose you are standing on the Skydeck of the Sears Tower in Chicago, 103 stories above the ground. As you look down, you see two cars turning a corner from opposite directions and about ready to collide. You know that they will crash into each other. But the knowledge of this event, which you have before it happens, does not control the crash. So it is with God. God's knowledge of events does not control our choices or destroy our freedom to live a full human life.

All-Present   God is everywhere. Another word for this attribute of God is *omnipresent*. To say that God is all-present does not mean that we need to make room for him on the seat next to us—as if we were talking about God as occupying space the way we do. God is present by the fact that he created everything and keeps everything in existence. Just as God is not limited by time, so God is not limited as we are by space. That is because God is a spirit. This means that God is not a material being; God is not made of matter and has no material parts.

Think about these attributes of God. Then choose one that is either especially important to you or especially difficult for you to understand. Write a prayer and talk to God about it.

CATHOLIC ID

Are you interested in taking care of God's creation? If so, you may wish to take Saint Francis of Assisi as your patron. He is the patron saint of all ecologists. Saint Francis reminded us that the created world is God's work of art. The all-powerful God filled it with value and beauty. As Catholics we should take the lead in caring for God's creation and never neglect it.

God is timeless, eternal. Someday we will share in his eternal life. Imagine what that will mean.

If God knows all things, how can we be truly free?

As a sign of respect for God's creation and for God our creator, get permission to sponsor an environmental day. Your group may want to take the lead in organizing something as simple as a clean-up day on the parish grounds.

YOU ARE MY WITNESSES

An author wrote that people's idea of God was too small. After reading this chapter, has your idea of God expanded or contracted?

Why do you think some people get upset when they learn from science that the world was not created by God in six or seven days? How would you explain the Catholic position on the creation of the world?

Find and define:

creator

_____

_____

_____

_____

THE GOD WHO IS

Worthy are you, LORD our God,
to receive glory and honor and power.

Revelation 4:11

HAVE you ever tried to picture God? Great artists such as Michelangelo pictured God as an older man with white hair and a beard. Does that sound like your picture of God, or is yours different?

Unlike Any Other

Our Old Testament ancestors in faith were forbidden to make any image of God. The reason for this is that God is a spirit. God also surpasses and goes beyond anything he has made. This surpassing excellence of God is called God's *transcendence*.

The ancient pagan gods were thought of as little more than superhuman beings. The biblical writers could never accept such a limited idea of the one true God. When they wrote of God, they wanted to stress the fact that God is totally different from us and the world around us. Think of the experience Moses had at the burning bush. When he began to approach the bush, God said, "Come no nearer! Remove the sandals from your feet" (Exodus 3:5). Moses stood trembling before the majesty of God. He knew that God was absolutely unlike any other being.

The most important word the biblical writers used to describe God's transcendence was the word *holy*. One of the most dramatic scenes in the Old Testament is based on the holiness of God. One day the prophet Isaiah went into the Temple of Jerusalem. There he had what he described as an overwhelming experience of God:

> I saw the Lord seated on a high and lofty throne, with the train of his garment filling the temple. Seraphim were stationed above; each of them had six wings: with two they veiled their faces, with two they veiled their feet, and with two they hovered aloft. "Holy, holy, holy is the LORD of hosts!" they cried one to the other. "All the earth is filled with his glory!" At the sound of that cry, the frame of the door shook and the house was filled with smoke.
> Isaiah 6:1–4

In magnificent images Isaiah attempts to share with us his experience of the transcendent God. God is pictured in great majesty, sitting on a throne. He is being worshiped and adored by the seraphim, six-winged creatures that often appeared in ancient Near Eastern art. In later times this heavenly court of God was identified with the angels. Using two of their wings, the seraphim covered their faces because no creature would dare to look upon God. Using two more wings, they covered their feet to keep a respectful distance from God. Finally, with the last two wings, they held themselves aloft as a way of showing God adoration and worship.

In Isaiah's scene the seraphim sing of God's holiness. They repeat the word *holy* three times to show that God is all holy, that God's holiness is endless. Only God is worthy of praise and complete adoration. God's *holiness* is another word for his otherness, his transcendence. God is completely apart from anything that he created. Isaiah highlighted this by concluding his vision of God's majesty with smoke filling the Temple. Smoke was a symbol for the presence of the transcendent God.

What are we to make of this scene from Isaiah? To say that God is holy means much more than the fact that God is good. Holiness is the essential characteristic of God. It tells us of his perfection, otherness, and total transcendence. God is completely apart from anything created; God is not one of his creatures.

God alone is holy. This statement may be surprising to those of us who think that we can be holy, too. But the source of all holiness is God. If we are holy, it is because we have been given a share in God's perfection. Our holiness is never our own; God alone is holy. Only he is worthy of our adoration and praise.

As we shall see, we have been called into a very intimate relationship with God. God is close to us. But we can never forget that God is transcendent. Otherwise we run the risk of thinking about God as only a creature like ourselves. Then to whom would we sing "holy, holy, holy"?

Have you ever had an experience of God's transcendence? Recall it. Write about it here or in your journal.

indirectly through angels. The very word *angel*, which means "messenger," tells us what these creatures of God do. Recall the story of the angel Raphael, who brought God's message of hope to a suffering family. He also offered the prayers of God's people in the presence of the transcendent God (Tobit 12:12–15).

Celebrating God's Grandeur

For thousands of years Catholics have used architecture and music to express their belief in the transcendence of God. Think of magnificent cathedrals soaring hundreds of feet into the air, built to praise God. The grandeur of architecture, stained glass, and music lifts our spirits to God.

Like the people of the Old Testament, we also think of God when we see the rising smoke and smell the fragrant fumes of incense, which we sometimes use at liturgy. As the psalmist says, "Let my prayer be incense before you; my uplifted hands an evening sacrifice" (Psalm 141:2).

The Old Testament celebrated God's transcendence in many ways. One way biblical writers expressed it was by writing about angels. In biblical times, God often revealed himself and acted

In the Old Testament we also find another way of expressing God's transcendence. This was done by substituting other words for the sacred name, Yahweh. This name was so holy that it was hardly ever spoken. The writers used terms such as the "face" of the Lord (Exodus 33:23), the "name" of the Lord (Exodus 20:24), and the "glory" of the Lord (1 Kings 8:11). This same devotion to God's name carried over into the New Testament. Matthew, for example, referred to the kingdom of heaven rather than the kingdom of God.

The Lord's Prayer sums up many Old Testament ideas about God's transcendence. It is significant that this prayer begins with the petition "hallowed be thy name." Here we are repeating the Old Testament practice of referring to God's name rather than referring directly to God.

In the opening address to God, we say "who art in heaven," suggesting that God is totally different from us. But at the same time we say "Our Father," reminding us of God's closeness to us. He who is in "heaven" and who is yet "Our Father" brings out the wonderful contrast between God's transcendence and God's nearness in our Christian experience.

Tell about those things that help you remember God's awesome transcendence, such as the vastness of space and a beautiful sunset.

Celebrating God's Closeness

Just as we speak of God's otherness by using the word *transcendence*, so we use another word when speaking of God's closeness to us. That word is *immanence*. We know that God is immanent, or close to us: "For what great nation is there that has gods so close to it as the LORD, our God, is to us whenever we call upon him?" (Deuteronomy 4:7).

The prophets constantly reminded the people of God's closeness. They did this by using very human images to show the closeness of God to his people. The prophet Hosea, for example, imagined God showing the love and tenderness of a parent, guiding his children in taking their first steps, lifting them in his arms, and healing their injuries (Hosea 11:3–4).

This nearness of God reaches its highest point in Jesus. God is so close to us in Jesus that Saint Paul writes, "You received a spirit of adoption, through which we cry, 'Abba, Father!'. . . We are children of God, and if children, then heirs, heirs of God and joint heirs with Christ. . . ." (Romans 8:15–17). How much more immanent, or close, can God be to us, his adopted children?

CATHOLIC TEACHINGS

About Angels

God created all things "seen and unseen." Catholics believe that angels are a part of this unseen creation. The Church teaches that all during life we are surrounded by the watchful care and intercession of the angels.

Angels are created spirits. This means they do not have material parts. They are also intelligent beings. Nevertheless they are still creatures, just as human beings are creatures. These messengers of God, who are mentioned again and again in the Old Testament, are spoken of frequently in the New Testament as well. For example, a multitude of angels, "the heavenly host," sang God's praises at the birth of Jesus (Luke 2:8–14). The Church celebrates two special feasts in honor of the angels: on September 29 (the Archangels Michael, Gabriel, and Raphael) and October 2 (the Guardian Angels).

Things to SHARE

What are some of the images used by Isaiah to share his experiences of the transcendent God?

Do you have any images of your own to describe your experiences of God? What are they?

OnLine WITH THE PARISH

At Mass this week you will pray:
Holy, holy, holy Lord, God
  of power and might,
heaven and earth are full
  of your glory.
  Hosanna in the highest.
You will also pray,
  Our Father, who art in heaven,
  hallowed be thy name.

Try to be aware at these moments that the all-holy transcendent God is also our Father and very close to us.

YOU ARE MY WITNESSES

Things to Think About

Were you surprised to find out that God alone is holy? What does this belief mean to you?

Imagine that you receive this message in your E-mail: "Words do not make a difference in the life of faith." Your response?

WORDS to REMEMBER

Find and define:

transcendence

_____

_____

_____

_____

THE TRIUNE GOD

Holy, holy, holy, Lord God Almighty!
All thy works shall praise thy Name,
in earth and sky and sea;
Holy, holy, holy, merciful and mighty,
God in three Persons, blessed Trinity!

Reginald Heber

WHEN Catholics renew their baptismal promises at Easter, the priest sprinkles the assembly with water blessed during the Easter Vigil. In response the congregation makes the sign of the cross.

In doing this, what are we professing about our belief in God?

Three interlocking rings, a symbol of the Trinity

The Blessed Trinity

What is the transcendent God really like?

After God gradually revealed himself over many centuries, humanity was finally given the most marvelous insight of all: God's people were introduced to the mystery of the Blessed Trinity. This is the central belief of Christian faith and life. By the *Blessed Trinity* we mean that there are three Persons in one God. The one and only God is Father, Son, and Holy Spirit.

What do we mean when we say that there are three Persons in one God? Are *Father*, *Son*, and *Holy Spirit* just different names for one and the same Being? Not at all! The Church teaches that the three Persons in the one God are distinct from one another and equal to one another. God is triune: three and one at the same time. God is not one with three parts; God is completely one and completely three.

66

We believe that the three Persons in one God are distinct from one another:

- The Father is not the Son or the Holy Spirit.
- The Son is not the Father or the Holy Spirit.
- The Holy Spirit is not the Father or the Son.

We also believe that these three Persons, who are distinct from one another, are equally God:

- The Father is God.
- The Son is God.
- The Holy Spirit is God.

 You may wish to use the accompanying chart to help you remember these ideas.

A Clear Understanding

It took a long time for Christians to work out these details about the Trinity. In their search for an understanding, the first Christians did not have a library of religion books from which they could get answers to their questions. An understanding of the Blessed Trinity had to be developed, and this took time.

During the third century a priest by the name of Arius made one of the first efforts to give a clear explanation of the Trinity. He tried his best but made a fundamental mistake and was in error.

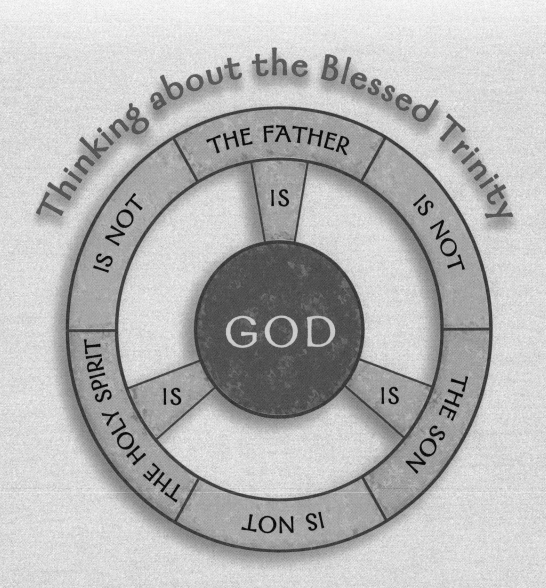

Thinking about the Blessed Trinity

THE FATHER
IS NOT
IS NOT
IS
GOD
IS
IS
THE SON
THE HOLY SPIRIT
IS NOT

Arius taught that God could not create the material world directly because God is transcendent. He would have to do this through someone else. That someone else was the Son. This meant, of course, that for Arius the Son was created and not transcendent; therefore the Son was not God. Look again at the chart to see why Arius was so wrong.

What was the reaction of the Church community? Arius' mistaken ideas began to spread, and a great controversy developed in the Church. People grew alarmed; even Emperor Constantine was concerned for the peace of his empire. That is why the bishops of the Church, who are responsible for correct doctrine, gathered in the city of Nicaea (in present-day Turkey) in A.D. 325.

It took the bishops a long time to work out and agree on the precise terms that would correctly define the doctrine of the Trinity for Catholics. To make it clear that the Son is God, just as the Father is God, the bishops said that the Son was "one in Being" with the Father. The teachings that emerged from the Council of Nicaea are the basis of the Nicene Creed, which we profess today at Mass. We, too, proclaim that the Son is "one in Being with the Father."

Why is it so important for us to know and understand all this? Does it have anything to do with our lives? It has everything to do with our lives! We have to be faithful to what God has revealed to us about himself. In order to do that, we must use the correct words. Some people think that words do not matter. People of faith know otherwise. And the more we get to know God, the more we will know of God's love for us.

Do you remember these words of Saint John: "God is love"? How does it make you feel to know that the triune God loves you? Write your thoughts in your journal.

Icon of the Blessed Trinity, Andrei Rublev, circa 1410

CATHOLIC ID

Catholics often refer to the "mysteries" of faith. A mystery is a truth of faith that we know only because God has revealed it to us. Human beings never fully understand a mystery. That is because only God, who is infinite, understands everything. However, it is the work of all believers to pray, study, and grow in understanding the mysteries of faith as much as they can. Think of this the next time you hear the words "Let us proclaim the mystery of faith" at Mass.

The Church and the Trinity

Almost everyone has heard the comparison of the Trinity to a shamrock, three leaves joined by one stem. This is certainly a clever way to approach the mystery of three in one. Another comparison is found in the legend of Saint Augustine at the seashore. According to the legend Augustine was watching a child trying to empty the vast ocean onto the shore, using a little sand bucket. When Augustine told the child that this was an impossible task, the child replied, "I'll finish this before you understand the Trinity."

Will we ever fully understand the Trinity? No. Otherwise we would be God. However, we have been privileged to get a glimpse of God's inner life. We are also privileged to live in relationship with God. The whole life of the Church, in fact, revolves around the Blessed Trinity. Catholics begin their prayers by making the sign of the cross. And the prayers of the liturgy are directed to God the Father, through the Son, in the Holy Spirit.

This is exactly what happens in the Mass and in the celebration of the sacraments. At Mass the eucharistic sacrifice of the Son is offered to the Father through the power of the Holy Spirit. Each of the sacraments also reminds us of the Trinity.

Before a person is baptized, for example, he or she is asked to profess belief in the Father, Son, and Holy Spirit. Three questions are asked, one for each Person of the Trinity. These are the same questions we are asked each year on Easter when we renew our baptismal promises.

What are the three questions asked at Baptism? Write them here.

Speaking About the Trinity

What sets Christianity apart from every other religion is belief in the Blessed Trinity. The early Christians were accused by some of practicing polytheism. Muslims and Jews alike have taken offense at the doctrine of the Trinity. They feel that if God is three, then God cannot be one. Of course we know that Christians do not believe in three gods. We believe in the triune God, three Persons in the one God.

Sometimes people try to speak about the Blessed Trinity without using the words *Father* and *Son*. They are worried that we may be thinking of God only in masculine terms, which would be wrong. Instead of the Father, Son, and Holy Spirit, they prefer creator, redeemer, and sanctifier.

The words *creator*, *redeemer*, and *sanctifier* are the traditional words used to describe the roles and works of the Persons of the Blessed Trinity. It is true to say that the Father is the creator, the Son is the redeemer, and the Holy Spirit is the sanctifier.

But using these words to replace the words *Father*, *Son*, and *Holy Spirit* can lead to misunderstanding.

Why is that? Because *Father*, *Son*, and *Holy Spirit* are words that show us a relationship among the three divine Persons. The words *creator*, *redeemer*, and *sanctifier* are not words of relationship. Rather they refer to God's work of creating, redeeming, and sanctifying; they do not tell us what God is. They are important but do not tell us about the inner life of God, which he has revealed to us.

What are we to think? It is important to remember that God is neither male nor female. God, who is spirit, has no gender. God's revelation to us, however, is clear: God is Father, Son, and Holy Spirit. We cannot change what God has told us.

Here is an easy way to remember and pray about this mystery of faith. Christians are baptized in the *name* of the Father and of the Son and of the Holy Spirit, not in their *names*. There is only one God, who is the Blessed Trinity.

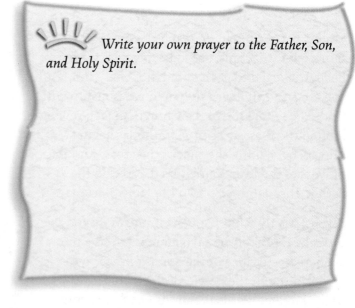

Write your own prayer to the Father, Son, and Holy Spirit.

Things to SHARE

Imagine that a non-Christian friend wants to know what Christians mean by the Blessed Trinity. What will you say?

A fourth-century Father of the Church, Saint Gregory of Nazianzus, wrote: "Above all guard for me this great deposit of faith, for which I live and fight, which I want to take with me as a companion . . . : I mean the profession of faith in the Father and the Son and the Holy Spirit. I entrust it to you today." What will you do with this great treasure entrusted to you?

OnLine WITH THE PARISH

At Mass, listen for these words of the eucharistic prayer:

Through him,
with him,
in him,
in the unity of the Holy Spirit,
all glory and honor is yours,
almighty Father,
for ever and ever.

Your firm response in the Great Amen will be an example of your belief in the Blessed Trinity.

YOU ARE MY WITNESSES

Things to Think About

Imagine you are a thoughtful Christian in the year 320. You have just heard the priest Arius give an explanation of the Trinity. How would you answer him?

Does the Blessed Trinity have anything to do with your life right now? Should it? Why?

Words to REMEMBER

Find and define:

Blessed Trinity

_____

_____

_____

_____

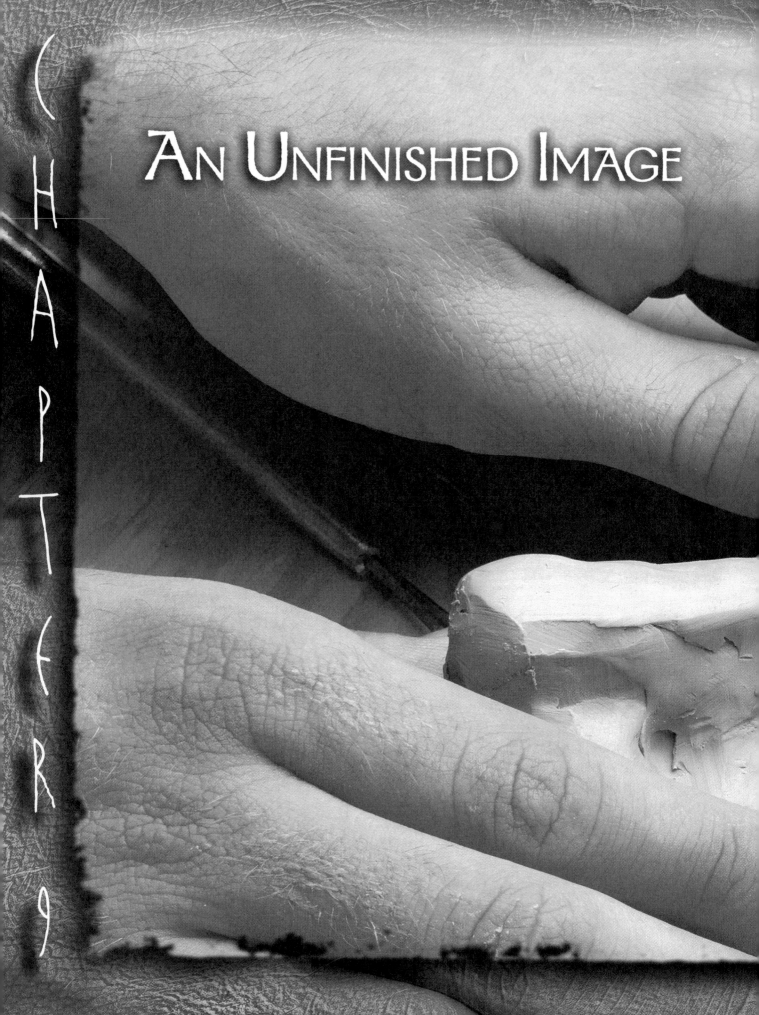

AN UNFINISHED IMAGE

CHAPTER 9

I praise you,
so wonderfully you made me;
wonderful are your works!

Psalm 139: 14

ON Ash Wednesday Christians have heard for centuries the words "Remember, you are dust, and to dust you will return." Dust! Is that all we are? Something to be blown away by the wind?

From the Dust of the Earth

Who are we? Where do we come from? Why are we here?

As people of faith we try to find out what God has revealed to us about human nature. It is important to discover not only what God has told us of himself but also what God has told us about ourselves. Because God is the source of all creation, the study of God and the study of the human person are like two sides of the same coin. We cannot study one without the other.

To help answer our questions, we turn to Genesis, which gives us the basis for our vision of human nature. Under the inspiration of the Holy Spirit,

the Genesis writers taught two important truths: that men and women are made in the image of God and that every human being has an immortal soul. These are the most basic truths that God revealed about us.

In God's Image   The first mention of humankind in Genesis is truly simple. It is that God created human beings in his image: "God created man in his image; in the divine image he created him; male and female he created them" (Genesis 1:27). Men and women were made in God's image. What does this mean?

The phrase *in God's image* tells us several important things. First, it tells us that God created Adam and Eve—the names of the first people in the Genesis story—as his friends. God shared the gift of divine life with them and with no other creatures on earth. Second, the phrase *in God's image* tells us that human beings were created with an intellect and a will. Like God we are intelligent beings; we can think and are free to choose.

Unlike plants and animals, human beings can know and love God. This is the reason we were created. And what is important to understand is that we know and love God freely. We are not forced. With this freedom we can choose to grow in the divine image in which we were created. Or we can choose to remain unfinished images.

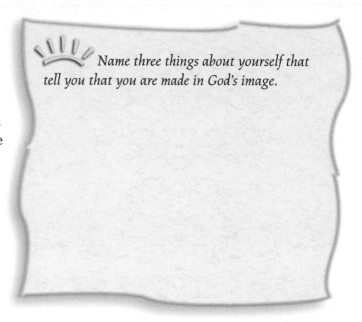

Name three things about yourself that tell you that you are made in God's image.

After teaching this startling truth about our human nature, the second chapter of Genesis continues with a symbolic and wonderfully imaginative description of humanity's creation. The biblical writers picture God as a sculptor forming the first human being from the dust of the earth, shaping clay and breathing life into it.

As strange as this poetic imagery may seem to modern, scientific minds, it should not be surprising. It was really based on the experience of ancient people. When they saw a dead body decay and turn to dust, they concluded that the human body was made and shaped from dust, the very elements of the earth. This may seem obvious, but it contains an extraordinary truth about human beings: Our bodies are made out of the same elements as the rest of creation. That connects us closely with the world around us and gives us reason to live as its responsible keepers.

An Immortal Soul

The Genesis writers pictured God the sculptor as putting his own life and breath into the first human being. Again, this was not a strange image for ancient peoples. After all, when a person stopped breathing, that person was dead. Breath meant life, as it does for us today. Just think of mouth-to-mouth resuscitation.

What did the biblical writers mean by the breath of life? In later times people thought of it as the soul. The *soul* is the spiritual part of every person; each of us has a soul created by God. Unlike the body, the soul has no parts. It is spiritual; it cannot die. That is why the soul is immortal.

Is the soul better than the body? Not really. We are a unity; we are body and soul. This is a truth that science cannot give us. This is a truth that only faith can provide.

Being an unfinished image isn't bad. It just means that we have to grow in God's image. What do you think the biggest challenge is in doing this?

Catholics and Evolution

Everyone is interested in the question of human origins. The topic is a concern of both religion and science. It is therefore important to know the truths about human origins found in the Bible and how they stack up against the findings of science.

To explain creation scientists speak of evolution. *Evolution* is a scientific theory; it states that higher forms of life evolved from lower forms of life. This theory has nothing to do with the truth of faith that God created everything. Nor does it upset the truth that we are a special part of God's creation.

Why is this so? Science and religion ask different kinds of questions; they look at the same truth from different points of view. On the one hand there is strong scientific evidence to support the theory that the human body evolved from a lower form of animal life. On the other hand Catholics believe that this was done according to a plan set in motion by the creator. Human beings are not simply the result of chance.

Scientists draw their conclusions from studying ancient civilizations and the remains of past human life. They also examine fossils found in different layers of the earth. All these studies give scientists reliable evidence that the human race has evolved over the centuries. Catholics respect this evidence.

When Catholics talk about the evolution of the human race, they are referring only to the body, never to the soul. Through science we know that the body is made up of material parts that can develop and evolve. But the soul is spiritual. It has no material parts and therefore is not subject to development and evolution.

Science, however, is not concerned with the study of the soul. Science leaves that to religion and theology. The Church teaches that God creates each human soul directly and immediately. The soul is not produced by parents. Unlike the human body, the soul is not the result of biological reproduction. It is spiritual and without parts. The soul is the result of a divine act, a direct act of God.

What can scientific study of fossils and rock layers and bones tell us about the evolution of the body? What can the study of these things tell us about the soul?

CATHOLIC TEACHINGS

About the Unity of Humanity

The creation of human beings as described in Genesis gives the basis for the Church's teaching about the unity of humanity: "Because of its common origin *the human race forms a unity*, for 'from one ancestor [God] made all nations to inhabit the whole earth'" (*Catechism*, 360). Catholics who take this teaching seriously can never participate in prejudice of any kind. People of every time and place are members of the same human race, and each person's soul is created directly by God.

Science and Faith

For Catholics there is no clash or conflict between Church teachings and what science tells us about evolution. Both are meant to bring us to the truth, and the truth is one. Thus Catholics may and do accept the theory that the human body evolved.

If you stop to think about it, we actually take evolution for granted in our everyday speech. We do not go around saying, "God created that rock, that tree, that river"—not directly, that is. God created in the beginning, and his creative act now works out according to the laws of nature that he put into matter at the dawn of creation. That includes our bodies. It is only the human soul that God must create directly.

Why is it so important to understand all these details about science and faith? Today some people rely only on science to answer life's mysteries and to solve all problems. This "science only" point of view is narrow-minded because it fails to recognize that the human person is both material and spiritual, body and soul. Science takes into account only the material part of humanity.

The real answers to the meaning of life take into account the whole human person, not just one part. That is why it is necessary to accept what we find in Scripture, as it is taught by the Church, together with the findings of science.

Some people go to the opposite extreme, however. They place their trust only in the Bible and ignore the insights of scientific study. Such a viewpoint is equally narrow-minded because it is based on a literal understanding of the Bible unacceptable to Catholics. As we saw in an earlier chapter, the Church teaches that the creation language of Genesis is richly symbolic. Taking it literally robs God of his attributes and forces upon God the limitations of a human artisan. A literal interpretation fails to recognize the splendor of God's intelligence and power that lies behind the process of evolution. Who but God could create in such an elaborate and magnificent way?

Someone tells you that you cannot accept the idea of evolution if you believe in the Bible. As a Catholic what is the first thing you would want to share with that person?

Archaeological dig

Some people say that the evolution of the human body is a terrible idea because it contradicts the Bible. What will you say to these people about the Catholic view of evolution?

You have an immortal soul. What does that mean to you?

OnLine WITH THE PARISH

Catholics who take seriously the Church's teaching about the unity of humanity are always aware of the evil of racial prejudice. Brainstorm with your group several ways you can campaign against prejudice in speech or in action. Then discuss ways you will share your campaign ideas with the rest of your parish.

YOU ARE MY WITNESSES

Things to Think About

Perhaps you have seen bumper stickers that read, "Be patient. God isn't finished with me yet." Name three ways in which you will cooperate with God in developing his unfinished image in you.

What does it mean to be made in God's image?

WORDS to REMEMBER

Find and define:

soul

_____

_____

_____

_____

79

A PROMISE OF HOPE

C
H
A
P
T
E
R

10

In all these things we conquer overwhelmingly through him who loved us.

Romans 8:37

THE old man is in his eighties now, but as he tells his story, his eyes show a horror as real today as when he first witnessed it as a twenty-one-year-old soldier.

In April 1945 an American armored division entered a Nazi concentration camp to free the prisoners and to provide medical aid. What they encountered there stunned and sickened them. The old soldier recalls hundreds of dead bodies thrown together in piles "like so many sticks." He saw the gas chambers and ovens in which thousands of others had been killed. Even sadder were the "walking dead," those who still lived but who were reduced almost to skeletons through starvation, illness, and forced labor.

The old man blinks to keep the tears back. "It is over fifty years ago," he says, "but I will never be able to forget what I saw. So much suffering. So much evil. Why?"

It is now estimated that over six million people, mostly Jews, were exterminated in the Nazi concentration camps. This terrible crime is called the Holocaust.

Can you answer the old soldier's question? Have you ever encountered evil or suffering that made you ask the same question? If God is good, how can there be such evil in the world?

Sin and Grace

Like everything in creation, the human race was created good. "God looked at everything he had made, and he found it very good" (Genesis 1:31). Made in God's image, human beings were given a share in God's own life at creation. This share in God's life we call sanctifying grace. *Sanctifying grace* is a participation in the very life of God that brings us into an intimate and permanent relationship with the Blessed Trinity. We first receive this divine gift at Baptism.

The idea of sanctifying grace is presented symbolically in the second and third chapters of Genesis. Adam and Eve are described as being in a beautiful garden, living in perfect happiness. There they had an easy friendship and personal relationship with God. This means that they were in the state of grace; they recognized their dependence on God and freely gave God their respect and trust. Then they were tested and given an opportunity to show their love for God. But by choosing freely to disobey him, our first parents proved themselves incredibly ungrateful for all that God had planned for them.

By disobeying God, Adam and Eve committed the first sin of humanity. We call this original sin. *Original sin* was the rejection of God by our first parents, resulting in the loss of sanctifying grace. With their sin Adam and Eve deprived themselves and all their descendants of the original state of grace given by God.

Down through the ages people have often referred to the sin of our first parents as "Adam's sin." So serious and deep was the wound of Adam's sin that it affected the whole human race. In the Genesis story Adam was the whole of humanity, along with Eve; and when he sinned, all humanity sinned in and with him. Thus all human beings are born in the state of original sin. Saint Paul was referring to

Scripture UPDATE

Scripture sometimes refers to "fallen angels" or "the devil." In 2 Peter 2:4 we read that "God did not spare the angels when they sinned." In 1 John 3:8 we read, "Whoever sins belongs to the devil, because the devil has sinned from the beginning." The Church's tradition understands in these references the existence of fallen angels, who embraced evil by their own doing. Such beings are creatures only and have no power over God.

humanity's sin through Adam when he wrote that just as "through one person sin entered the world, and through sin, death," so death came to all of us because all sinned in Adam (Romans 5:12).

The Effects of Original Sin

Original sin was a rejection of God. The story of Adam and Eve's sin indicated their pride and refusal to obey God; they put their own desires and will before God's will. Their rejection of God's will ended with the loss of sanctifying grace, resulting in an emptiness and absence.

When we say that we are born with original sin, we are not talking about a personal sin we have committed. We mean that we are born without sanctifying grace. We share the same emptiness and absence of grace that all humanity has suffered since the sin of our first parents. That is the reason the Church teaches that infants are to be baptized as soon as possible. Baptism restores us to the original state of grace given to humanity.

Besides losing sanctifying grace, our first parents lost other privileges when they sinned. From the Genesis story we know that the whole human race is forever subject to the following effects of original sin:

- *Ignorance:* As everyone knows, learning does not always come easily.
- *Suffering:* Suffering and pain are part of life. We cannot escape them.
- *Inclination to evil:* Like Adam and Eve we are tempted to see evil as good and are tempted to reject God.
- *Death:* Because of sin, human beings cannot escape death, either.

As members of the human race, we inherit the effects of Adam's sin. This is a great mystery. Although we are not personally responsible for Adam's sin, each one of us who sins agrees with the choice of Adam. We, too, freely and personally join Adam in his rebellion against God.

We often refer to the free decision of Adam and Eve to turn away from God as "the fall." The free choice that was made by the first human beings to sin against God resulted in a "fallen" human nature. The human race has fallen from the close relationship with God that God first intended for us. In this fallen state, however, humanity is not totally lost. Human nature has been wounded and weakened but did not become totally evil or totally corrupted. God's creation is still good, but it is in need of a share in the divine life, in need of sanctifying grace.

Make a list of some current events that might help to explain the Church's teaching on original sin.

Can you name some effects of original sin?

God's Promise

There are some people in the world who do not believe in sin at all, much less original sin. They try to explain it away. But they cannot do so, not if they are honest. All they have to do is look at the evening news on television or read the daily paper. The results of original sin are all around us. We are far from being perfect creatures, and this certainly makes original sin an easy doctrine to accept.

If human beings freely chose to commit original sin at the dawn of human history, then humanity itself is the cause of sin and evil in the world. God is not the cause of evil. He created everything good. God did not force the first human beings to commit sin.

It was their free choice to disobey their creator. Human beings are the ones who have turned good into evil by their own choice. This is a revealed truth of our faith.

Is humanity therefore without hope? Is fallen human nature beyond repair? What do you think?

Some people have held that we are in a hopeless state, but that is not the Catholic view. The Church teaches that even though human beings abused their freedom by choosing to sin, God did not abandon them. This is clearly seen in the story of Adam and Eve as it unfolds in the third chapter of Genesis. According to that account our first parents were tempted by a serpent, the symbol of evil, to disobey God. Adam and Eve chose disobedience. But before God expelled them from the garden, a symbol of their loss of sanctifying grace, he held out a promise to them. That promise is contained in a statement that God made to the serpent, the tempter:

> I will put enmity between you and the woman,
>   and between your offspring and hers;
> He will strike at your head,
>   while you strike at his heel.
> Genesis 3:15

What does this statement mean? Catholics have understood it as the first promise of salvation given by God. As we look at this verse, we are able to see the fulfillment of God's promise in Jesus. The reason for this is that we have the advantage of reading this promise from a New Testament point of view. It is not difficult to look back now to the opening chapters of Genesis and read into them what we know: that Jesus' passion, death, and resurrection brought the saving victory over sin and evil. Evil would not have the last word.

Loved by God

What about the woman mentioned in the verse? Obviously it is Eve. But Catholics also think of another woman when they read Genesis 3:15. We think of Mary, the mother of Jesus, as the woman whose offspring would put his "heel" on the serpent and crush its "head." What a beautiful and hope-filled promise we have in this verse! It has often been called the first announcement of the good news of salvation.

Scripture and tradition picture Jesus as the "new Adam," who overcame the faults of the first Adam. Instead of the emptiness and absence of grace left to us by Adam, Jesus, the new Adam, brings us an overflow of divine life and grace. As Saint Paul wrote, "For just as in Adam all die, so too in Christ shall all be brought to life" (1 Corinthians 15:22).

One of the great truths of our faith is that human beings are good even though we are flawed by original sin. Original sin did not make human nature evil but did weaken it. As a result we have to work constantly against the effects of original sin in our lives. These include fear, jealousy, pride, selfishness—all the things that make human beings less than what God created us to be. And this struggle will continue our whole lives, even with the help of God's grace. The doctrine of original sin, therefore, is not only about something that happened a long time ago. It also tells us about ourselves today.

Even with original sin we are still loved by God. And human beings have been given almost unimaginable capabilities. Think of the wonderful things we can do, what great thoughts we can think. We have even landed on the moon! And what is most exciting, we have been called to participate in God's very life. What a marvelous creature is a human being that God would even think to become one of us at the incarnation!

Give an example for this statement: Even though human beings have been weakened by original sin, we are still good.

Things to SHARE

What can give us confidence that evil will not have the last word in our lives?

A family you know is about to celebrate the Baptism of a new baby. The parents have a problem with the idea of original sin. They say to you, "It's unfair. Our baby never did anything wrong." Your response?

OnLine WITH THE PARISH

How does your parish proclaim that Jesus' passion, death, and resurrection brought the saving victory over sin and evil? How can young people become part of that proclamation? How can *you* become a sign of hope to others?

YOU ARE MY WITNESSES

Things to Think About

In what ways do you see the effects of original sin in your own life?

Then consider what you have learned about the Catholic view of human nature. Is it more fitting for a Catholic to be an optimist or a pessimist about life?

WORDS to REMEMBER

Find and define:

original sin

_____

_____

_____

_____

THE PERFECT IMAGE

CHAPTER 11

For my eyes have seen your salvation,
a light for revelation to the Gentiles,
and glory for your people Israel.

Luke 2:30, 32

THERE are no photographs of him. He never wrote a book or traveled far from the place where he was born. Yet he is supposed to be the center of our lives. This is Jesus of Nazareth. What do we know about him?

Nazareth today

The Fullness of Time

It was the fullness of time. The Roman Empire stretched from Spain and Britain in the west to Palestine and Syria in the east. It was a time of peace, with law and order assured by Roman soldiers stationed throughout the empire. For the first time in human history, good roads went everywhere. Never before had so many nations been united in one empire.

There was still unrest, however. Many of the proud peoples from different countries and cultures of the Roman Empire hated the foreign forces that occupied their lands. In Palestine the Jews were especially unhappy. King Herod, a Jew, had been appointed by Rome, but he was not the king the Jews wanted, one from the line of King David.

Instead they looked forward even more toward the coming of the Messiah, the promised one. Some thought he would be a great military leader who would protect them from their enemies and expel the hated foreign invaders. There was restlessness in the air. And then the time arrived. "When the fullness of time had come, God sent his Son, born of a woman" (Galatians 4:4).

Jesus was born without any display or fanfare. Mary was his virgin mother; and Joseph, his foster father, was a descendant of King David. Mary and Joseph had gone to the little town of Bethlehem to be registered in the Roman census. Every citizen of the empire had to register so that the emperor would have an accurate count for tax purposes. It was in Bethlehem that Jesus was born. In the great empire of Rome, he was just another statistic in the census.

After eight days the child born of Mary was named Jesus. The name *Jesus* means "God saves." Very little is known of Jesus' childhood and early life in Nazareth. Luke sums it up in one verse: "Jesus advanced in wisdom and age and favor before God and man" (Luke 2:52).

Even though we have no record of his childhood, we do know from many sources what life must have been like at the time of Jesus. Like the other boys of Nazareth, Jesus probably attended the local synagogue school. It seems clear that he did not set himself apart from the other young people of his town. He was not wealthy. He grew up just as everyone else did.

When Jesus was about thirty years old and ready to begin his public preaching, people barely noticed him. As he approached John the Baptist to be baptized in the Jordan River, John told the crowd, "There is one among you whom you do not recognize" (John 1:26). But John recognized Jesus! So John pointed to him and said, "Behold, the Lamb of God, who takes away the sin of the world" (John 1:29). With these words John the Baptist was comparing Jesus to the lamb used at Passover: Jesus was to shed his blood like a sacrificial lamb.

John's baptism was not like the sacrament of Baptism we have today. It was a ritual of repentance, a sign that people wanted to change their lives. Although Jesus had no need of repentance, he asked for John's baptism. In this way Jesus would identify himself with the rest of humanity. Then, at the moment of baptism, a startling event took place:

"On coming up out of the water he [Jesus] saw the heavens being torn open and the Spirit, like a dove, descending upon him. And a voice came from the heavens, 'You are my beloved Son; with you I am well pleased'" (Mark 1:10–11).

It might appear from Mark's Gospel that everyone present at Jesus' baptism heard a voice from heaven and saw the Holy Spirit descend upon Jesus. That is not so. Jesus alone saw and heard the heavenly happenings. In that moment he was set apart for his ministry, his Father's work. During the rest of his life on earth, Jesus would gradually reveal himself as both God and Man.

If you were an artist, how would you picture Jesus? How would you want people to see him?

Jesus pictured as the Lamb of God on an ivory book cover

*Detail from **Coronation of the Virgin**, Diego Rodríguez Velázquez, 1641–1642*

In the Beginning

At the very heart and life of Christian faith is Jesus of Nazareth. He is the most unique individual in human history. Why is this so? To answer this question, Christians turn to the earliest communities who knew Jesus and were closest to him. What do they tell us about his coming to our world? Most talk about his birth at Bethlehem, using wonderful stories of faith to help us understand him. But one gospel in particular gets right to the core of Jesus' identity in a way unlike any other. This is the Gospel of John, in which Jesus is called the "Word," who came to earth to live with us.

The *Word* is the name for the second Person of the Blessed Trinity in Saint John's Gospel. Why did John use this name, the *Word*? He was reminding us of a wonderful truth: that through words we express the deepest part of ourselves. This is true of God as well. By calling the second Person of the Trinity the *Word*, John was telling us that the Word is the deepest expression of God himself. In John's Gospel we read:

> In the beginning was the Word,
> and the Word was with God,
> and the Word was God.
> John 1:1

In three simple clauses John tells us three important truths:

- The Word, the second Person of the Blessed Trinity, always existed; the Word was already there at the start of creation.
  - The Word was present with God but was distinct from him. (Remember, the Son is not the Father.)
  - The Word was divine. The Word was distinct from God, but the Word was also God, sharing the same divine nature.

Later in the first chapter of John's Gospel we read, "And the Word became flesh and made his dwelling among us" (John 1:14). In this verse John tells us that the Word came to earth to live *with us*. John had already told us about the Word's divinity, that the Word was *God*. Here John speaks of the Word as *human*. The Word has become flesh, a frail mortal, taking on a human nature like our own.

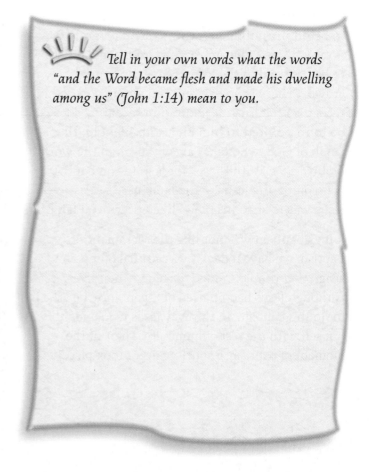

Tell in your own words what the words "and the Word became flesh and made his dwelling among us" (John 1:14) mean to you.

92

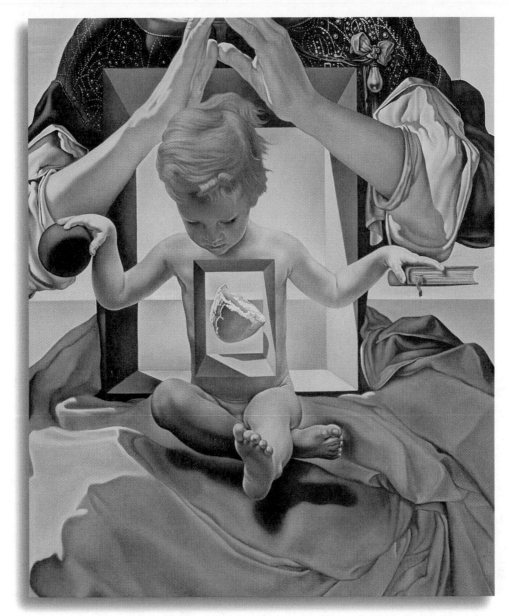

Detail from **Madonna of Port Lligat**, 1950, Salvador Dalí's symbolic representation of the incarnation reminding us that Jesus is the Bread of Life

The Incarnation

The taking on of flesh by the Word is not an easy idea to understand. As used by John, *Word* refers to a "Person," to the God-Man Jesus Christ. God reveals himself to us in this Word. Jesus is God's message to us in the flesh.

To describe this great event, we talk about the *incarnation*, a word meaning "the putting on or taking on of flesh." Christians define the *incarnation* as the union of divinity with humanity in Jesus Christ. It is the mystery of the second Person of the Blessed Trinity becoming one of us, the mystery of Jesus Christ being God and Man. Jesus is the Word of God made flesh.

There is a great deal to think about here. Jesus is truly divine and truly human. He is not God disguised as a human or God wearing a human mask. Jesus is one of us, with a human soul and body like ours. To all who knew him in Galilee and Judaea, he was the man Jesus. He got hungry and thirsty; he grew tired. Sometimes he was happy, sometimes sad. He knew fear, loneliness, and discouragement. He perspired in the heat and shivered in the cold. He went fishing and got his hands dirty. He was one of us in all things except this: He was sinless. Nevertheless, in becoming fully human, he did not stop being God. That is why the early Church could proclaim, "He is the image of the invisible God" (Colossians 1:15), the perfect image of the Father.

Although this teaching of the Church about the incarnation is very clear today, it was not always so. Some Christians in the early Church held that Jesus only *appeared* to be human. They said that it was unworthy of God to become incarnate with a human body and to live, suffer, and die.

Today we know that these people were wrong. The Church teaches that Jesus *was truly* a man. He did not *just appear* to be a man. He was not God in a human disguise. That is why a New Testament writer could truthfully say that he had heard, had seen with his own eyes, and had touched with his hands the Word of life (1 John 1:1–3).

 Do you think people need to know more about Jesus' divinity or his humanity? Explain.

CATHOLIC ID Ignatius of Antioch, one of the Fathers of the Church, taught clearly about the humanity of Jesus. In A.D. 110 he wrote, "Do not listen when anyone speaks to you apart from Jesus Christ, who was of the race of David, who was the son of Mary, who was truly born and ate and drank, was truly persecuted under Pontius Pilate, was truly crucified and died" (*Letter to the Trallians*, 9).

What do we mean when we say that Jesus came in the fullness of time? Describe "fullness of time."

What does the name *Jesus* mean? What significance does that meaning have for you?

Take a few moments this week to do your own gospel sketch of Jesus. Choose any of the four gospel accounts. Then make a list of all the wonderful human qualities you see in Jesus our friend and brother. Use this list as your own litany of thanksgiving to Jesus. For example, you might say, "Jesus, you cared for those in need. Help me to do the same."

Combine your litanies. Offer them to your pastor as a Prayer of the Faithful for Mass.

YOU ARE MY WITNESSES

Someone says to you, "Jesus could never know what it's like to be me or know how I feel. Besides, he had all the answers. He didn't have to work at anything!" What is your response as a Catholic?

In John's Gospel, the second Person of the Trinity is called the *Word*. Why did John use this name?

Find and define:

the Word

_____

_____

_____

_____

THE WORD MADE FLESH

THE WORD MADE FLESH

And the Word became flesh
and made his dwelling among us.

John 1:14

WHO are the people who have had an impact on your life? Is it someone whose music is at the top of the charts? Is it an athlete whose skills astonish you or someone who is a computer genius? Perhaps it is an artist or a poet or an author. Or maybe it is simply someone who has loved and cared for you in a special way.

What makes a person memorable and real in your eyes? What makes a person worth your admiration and your imitation? In other words, why do you want to know that person and to have him or her in your life?

Is the name of Jesus on your list?

Jesus of Nazareth

What can we possibly know about Jesus of Nazareth, who lived two thousand years ago? Did he really exist? As people of faith our answer is, "Of course!" Nevertheless nonbelievers may say, "What proof do you have?"

What would your answer to that question be? Are the faith statements we call the New Testament our only source of knowing whether or not Jesus even existed? The answer is no. There are a number of ancient historical sources that verify and support the existence of Jesus.

In Josephus One of the most famous nonbiblical sources that refers to Jesus comes from a Jewish historian who died at the end of the first century. His name was Flavius Josephus. Here is what he wrote about Jesus and his followers:

> At this time there appeared Jesus, a wise man…. For he was a doer of startling deeds, a teacher of people who received the truth with pleasure. And he gained a following both among many Jews and among many of Greek origin…. And when Pilate, because of an accusation made by the leading men among us, condemned him to the cross, those who had loved him previously did not cease to do so…. And up until this very day the tribe of Christians, named after him, has not died out.
> *Antiquities of the Jews*, vol. 18

In Tacitus Among several pagan Roman writers, we can read the words of the Roman historian Tacitus. He wrote about the great fire in Rome during the reign of the emperor Nero in A.D. 64. Nero was afraid of rumors that he had set the great fire himself. Tacitus wrote:

> To squelch the rumor, Nero created scapegoats and subjected to the most refined tortures those whom the common people called "Christians," hated for their abominable crimes. Their name

comes from Christ, who, during the reign of Tiberius, had been executed by the procurator Pontius Pilate. Suppressed for the moment, the deadly superstition broke out again, not only in Judaea, the land which originated this evil, but also in the city of Rome.

Annals, 15, 44

There is no doubt that when Tacitus wrote these words in A.D. 115 he was not a lover of Christianity, since he calls it an evil and a superstition. He certainly knows about the place from which Christianity comes and about its founder. However, from Tacitus, as well as from Josephus and other nonbiblical writers, it is clear that Jesus was not simply an idea dreamed up by someone.

 In what ways was Jesus truly human like us?

In the Gospels Our most valuable sources for information about Jesus of Nazareth are the gospel accounts. Of course they were never meant to be like modern history textbooks. But they are based on what really happened in history. The gospels are important because they give us the meaning of this history for our faith.

From the gospels we learn that Jesus grew up in Nazareth of Galilee and was known as the Nazarene. People were not amazed at his unusual abilities: As a baby he did not talk in the manger; as a child he did not work miracles. He had to grow in knowledge as we do. He did not have automatic answers to life's problems. Despite what some people or some artists might envision, Jesus had not been a full-grown man living in heaven from all eternity who shrank into a baby before entering Mary's womb.

Growing up in the Galilean hills, Jesus had to learn many things about life. Although he was a carpenter by trade, his speech and understanding of life were influenced by the farming communities of the area and all that farmers experience. He knew about vineyards and growing grapes, as well as about the daily wages of farmers.

When Jesus was sick, he had to take medicine and rest. He enjoyed being with his friends and no doubt engaged in the sports of his day. Without a telephone, television, or computer, Jesus learned many things from listening to his family, relatives, and the people of the village as they discussed the problems of everyday life. Jesus even had to learn how to pray. When we look at the life of Jesus of Nazareth, we see that he lived a normal life.

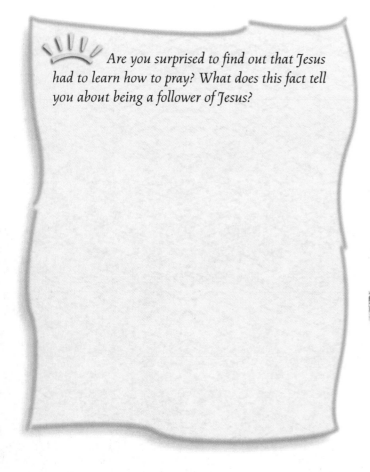

Are you surprised to find out that Jesus had to learn how to pray? What does this fact tell you about being a follower of Jesus?

Laughing Jesus,
Nuñez Segura, 1988

Jesus the Man

When it happened, we do not know exactly. But one day Jesus left his hometown of Nazareth and began what we now call his public life. It was time for him to bring the good news to others. So he set out on a journey throughout Palestine. This journey, however, was not going to be a long one. It would last only about three years.

Galilee today

Likable The gospels clearly picture Jesus as a likable friend, searching people out. Wherever people were, he went to them: their homes, the streets, the marketplace. Jesus did not keep a distance from others but was involved in their everyday lives. That is why he attended wedding feasts, banquets, and other gatherings to which he was invited.

Jesus must have been easy to talk with. He shared himself with his friends, as all friends do. He rejoiced with them when things were going well, wept with them when they were sad. He visited their homes and sometimes stayed overnight, as he did with Zacchaeus (Luke 19:1–10). No one was a stranger to Jesus. His friends included the rich and the poor, the young and the old, the popular and the unpopular. He knew shepherds and how they felt looking for a stray sheep. He could sympathize with a housewife who had lost some money.

Jesus went out of his way for those who were sick or in need, even for those who were outcasts and hated by others. Though Jesus was compassionate, he was not a weakling. Discouraged at times, he never gave up. Rejected, he went back to his task again and again. Hated, he loved in return. Not that he was without feeling. He had moments of anger (Matthew 21:12–13) and loneliness, too.

The gospel accounts of Matthew, Mark, Luke, and John are for the most part concerned with the public life and message of Jesus, what he did and what he said. If we take these gospels and put them together, we can begin to draw a sketch of the man Jesus. Certainly the gospels do not provide us with everything there is to know about him; this was not their purpose. But they do give us a definite impression of Jesus' life and the kind of individual he was.

During the years of his public life, Jesus made many friends—and enemies, too. But no matter what people may have thought of him, Jesus was an exciting and impressive individual. Here was a man who had come to know what life was all about. Those who believed in him and followed him found a new purpose in living. They said, "Never before has anyone spoken like this one" (John 7:46).

Scripture UPDATE

One of the shortest verses in Scripture eloquently describes the humanity of Jesus. It does so in three words: "And Jesus wept" (John 11:35). Jesus had just gone to see the burial place of his friend Lazarus. Jesus' love for his friend was so great that he cried. What deeper expression of human emotion is there?

Concerned for Everyone To those who followed him, Jesus spoke boldly about God's place in their lives. He called them to be his disciples and to turn to God. One of the things we can admire most in the man Jesus is his strong determination. He was misunderstood by many but never changed what he knew he had to do or say. Even in the face of opposition, he continued to teach with authority.

Perhaps the best way we can identify with Jesus as a friend is to see the way he treated people. He enjoyed them. Somehow we can tell when others like us. The apostles felt that same warmth with Jesus. With little hesitation they decided to join him (Mark 1:16–20) and became the Twelve. And with the Twelve, Jesus was a thoughtful friend, too. Once, after the apostles had spent a full day on the road, Jesus invited them to take a break. He said, "Come away by yourselves to a deserted place and rest a while" (Mark 6:31).

With his disciples gathered close to him, Jesus was filled with joy and sought out those who were thought to be "lost." Some people complained about him, "This man welcomes sinners and eats with them" (Luke 15:2). But these sinners were the ones with whom Jesus wanted to spend his time; they were the ones who needed him most.

Jesus also treated women differently than was customary. Unlike other teachers Jesus welcomed women among his followers. Together with the Twelve some women accompanied Jesus on his travels (Luke 8:1–3). Still others were taught by Jesus, as Martha and Mary were (Luke 10:38–42).

This gospel sketch of Jesus shows us a man who came to know exactly who he was. Full of love, Jesus was ready to face anything in life. He was fully alive and fully human. But this is only half the story. As the incarnation reminds us, he was also divine, the Son of God.

Which gospel passage helps you to remember that Jesus is your friend, too? Write your thoughts in your journal.

CATHOLIC TEACHINGS

About Jesus' Humanity

The Church never wants us to forget that Jesus was a Jew. He was born into a Jewish family and grew up practicing the Jewish religion. He cherished the traditions of his ancestors and worshiped God in the local synagogue and at the Temple in Jerusalem. To forget that Jesus was a Jew is to forget an essential part of his humanity.

A recent drawing of Jesus shows him laughing and having fun. Some people think that it might be disrespectful to show Jesus this way. What would you say about it?

The gospels portray Jesus as a true and loving friend, someone who was concerned about others. How can you imitate the concern of Jesus by helping out in your parish community? Find out what helping organizations exist in your parish. Then discover how you might become a part of their ministry.

YOU ARE MY WITNESSES

Things to Think About

What have you learned about Jesus that makes you want to know him better? How will you go about doing that?

WORDS to REMEMBER

Find and define:

Nazareth

_____

_____

_____

_____

CHAPTER 13

MESSIAH, LORD, AND SAVIOR

We adore you,
O Christ, and we praise you
because by your holy cross
you have redeemed the world.

WHAT was the purpose of Jesus' life?
Was he just a great teacher, a bearer of good news?
What difference has he made in our world?

Words Filled with Meaning

The birth of Jesus was like no other. That is why his coming was announced to shepherds by an angel who said, "Do not be afraid; for behold, I proclaim to you good news of great joy that will be for all the people. For today in the city of David a savior has been born for you who is Messiah and Lord" (Luke 2:10–11).

With a few simple words, Luke gives us a most important message about the meaning of Jesus' life: that he is Messiah, Lord, and Savior. What does each of these words mean?

Messiah   The word *messiah* is a Hebrew word meaning "anointed one." When this word was translated by the early Church into Greek, the word became *Christos*, or *Christ*. *Messiah* and *Christ*, therefore, mean the same thing.

Messiah was a very important word for God's people in Old Testament times. The word reminded them that priests, kings, and prophets were anointed with oil. When a king was enthroned, for example, oil was poured over his head. This meant that he was being set apart from all others and was responsible to God alone.

By the time of Jesus, there was no longer a king of Israel from the family of King David. Many people thought that the Messiah would come from that family as a king and warrior who would make Israel a great world power. Surely, they thought, this was God's promise to the chosen people.

Jesus, however, did not think this way. In fact he never called himself the Messiah. He did not want to give the impression that he agreed with the mistaken idea of the Messiah as a worldly king or warrior. For Jesus, the Messiah was to be a servant of God who would change the world by his suffering. The first Christians realized that Jesus was this Messiah, this suffering servant of God. They called him the Christ and therefore regarded Jesus as the true Messiah of Israel. Nevertheless, as Christianity spread throughout the world, other titles, such as "Lord" and "Savior," were used to describe who Jesus really was.

Lord   In Old Testament times the transcendent God, Yahweh, was referred to as the Lord. Using *Lord* for *Yahweh* was a sign of respect. So *Yahweh* (*God*) and *Lord* meant the same thing. Because Jesus was the Son of God—human and divine—he, too, was Lord. In fact the earliest expression of Christian faith was "Jesus Christ is Lord" (Philippians 2:11).

Savior   Just like the word *Lord*, the word *Savior* was used in the Old Testament to describe God. Because God rescued people from sin and death, he was frequently called Savior. We see this in the writings of the prophet Isaiah, for example. There God says, "For I am the LORD, your God, the Holy One of Israel, your savior" (Isaiah 43:3).

The work of the Savior is to bring salvation to the world. *Salvation* means "to heal," or "to be made whole." In Luke 2:10–11 Jesus, whose very name means "God saves," is announced to all as the Savior of the world. Jesus would restore the relationship that God had planned to share with humanity before original sin.

The salvation that Jesus gives is a healing from sin. It is sin that separates humanity from God. The goal of Jesus' life was to restore what God originally intended: that there be an intimate relationship between God and humanity and among people themselves. How could this be done? It would take someone who had the power of God to accomplish this, someone who was himself both God and Man. That Person was Jesus Christ our Lord.

Jesus our Savior brings healing to the world. Where do you think Jesus' healing is most needed today?

A Divine Person

Throughout his life Jesus acted as someone with authority, doing what only God could do. The early Church professed its faith in this divinity of Jesus by saying "Jesus is the Son of God."

The people of Jesus' time knew that only God can forgive sins. No one but God can heal the break with God that sin causes in our lives. Nevertheless Jesus, the man from Nazareth, took it upon himself to forgive sins. He did this over and over again. In fact Jesus said that love of him wins forgiveness for sins. This was his message to the woman who showed great love for him. He said to her, "Your sins are forgiven" (Luke 7:48). This is the same message of love Jesus shares with us.

Jesus did other things that only a divine Person can do. One day some people tried to insult Jesus as he was speaking to them. When Jesus referred to Abraham in a close and familiar way, his listeners questioned him, saying, "You are not yet fifty years old and you have seen Abraham?" Jesus replied, "Amen, amen, I say to you, before Abraham came to be, I AM" (John 8:57, 58).

By calling himself I AM, Jesus was using the name God had revealed to Moses. When Moses had asked what God's name was, God said, "This is what you shall tell the Israelites: I AM sent me to you" (Exodus 3:14). By using the words I AM, Jesus was making himself an equal of Yahweh.

Christ Redempteur, *Giraudon, 1393–94*

One day Jesus gave a glimpse of his divinity to the apostles Peter, James, and John at the transfiguration. In a brief moment Jesus' "face shone like the sun and his clothes became white as light." Then the apostles heard a voice saying, "This is my beloved Son, with whom I am well pleased; listen to him" (Matthew 17:2, 5). In this vision Jesus was letting his apostles know just how close he was with God the Father. At another time Jesus would tell the people, "The Father and I are one" (John 10:30).

 Give three examples from Jesus' life that show he was divine.

Worker of Miracles

The miracles of Jesus were signs of his divine power. Jesus raised the dead to life, gave sight to the blind, cured lepers, opened the ears of the deaf, enabled the lame to walk, and loosened the tongues of those who could not speak. Jesus also calmed the stormy sea and fed thousands on the hillside with just a few loaves of bread and pieces of fish.

Although Jesus worked many miracles, he did not make a show of his power. Filled with divine love and compassion, he even asked that his miraculous power be kept secret. One day a leper came to him. Calling Jesus "Lord," the leper asked to be cured.

CATHOLIC TEACHINGS

About the Person of Christ

In the early Church the following question arose: After the incarnation was Jesus two persons, a divine person and a human person? Or was he one person, and if so, a human person or a divine person? The followers of Nestorius, the bishop of Constantinople, mistakenly thought that Jesus was a human person in whom God was housed. This implied that Jesus was two persons: a divine person and a human person—like putting flowers in a vase (a divine person inside a human person).

To set things straight Nestorius himself asked that a Church council answer the question. The Council of Ephesus was called in A.D. 431. That council, as well as the Council of Chalcedon in A.D. 451, condemned any teaching that would split Christ into two persons. Ever since that time the Church has clearly taught that Jesus is one Person: a divine Person with two natures (a divine nature and a human nature). At the incarnation the second Person of the Trinity took on a human nature, not another person.

After Jesus cured him, he said to the leper, "See that you tell no one, but go show yourself to the priest, and offer the gift that Moses prescribed" (Matthew 8:4). Why did Jesus say this?

It was not out of a sense of false humility that Jesus asked for secrecy. He did not want people to become obsessed with the idea of power and think of him only as a miracle worker. Jesus wanted them to listen to his message. That is why he said, "Blessed are those who hear the word of God and observe it" (Luke 11:28).

The miracles of Jesus fill us with wonder, but they are not the cornerstones of our faith. Those who have faith in Jesus are able to believe in him only because faith is a God-given gift. It is true that miracles can lead people to believe, but they cannot produce faith. Faith is God's gift to those who freely accept his word. We accept God on his terms because it is God who is speaking.

What do the words of Jesus from Luke 11:28 tell you about being a disciple today? Write your response here or in your journal.

Someone says, "Wouldn't it be better if Jesus would keep on working miracles so that more people would believe in him?" What would you answer?

OnLine WITH THE PARISH

Make a visit to your parish Church. Look around carefully. What do you find there that reminds you that Jesus is Lord? that Jesus is the Son of God?

YOU ARE MY WITNESSES

Things to Think About

Why do you think that Jesus, the Messiah, did not make a show of his miraculous power?

What is the salvation that Jesus our Savior brings us?

Words to Remember

Find and define:

Savior

_____

_____

_____

_____

CHAPTER 14

MY LORD AND MY GOD

No one has greater love than this,
to lay down one's life for one's friends.

John 15:13

FORMER basketball star and Hall of Famer Oscar Robertson was in the news again—but not for basketball. His daughter, desperately ill with a disease that was destroying her kidneys, needed a transplant to survive. Robertson told the doctors that he wanted to be the donor; he would give one of his kidneys to save his daughter's life. The operation was performed, and the outcome was guarded but very hopeful.

A reporter asked the basketball great what had motivated him to make such a sacrifice. "I'm a father," was his reply.

Do you understand Robertson's response? What does sacrifice mean to you? What do you think was the greatest sacrifice of all?

The Lamb of God

Although Jesus himself was sinless, he freely chose to take upon himself the sins of the world. That is why Jesus was willing to be condemned to death as a common criminal, to be crowned with thorns, and to carry his own cross to Calvary. His acceptance of his passion and death was a completely selfless act. "No one has greater love than this, to lay down one's life for one's friends" (John 15:13).

Because of his great love, Jesus was willing to die for us and to offer to God the sacrifice of his own life. Death was the result of sin, and Jesus met death head on. Because he embraced our human life totally, Jesus really experienced death and all the pain and sorrow that surround it. This was the perfect sacrifice, the only one that would reconcile humanity with God. Through his death and resurrection, Jesus enabled all people to pass over from death to a whole new life with God. This is what we call our redemption and why Jesus is our redeemer.

Can you imagine choosing to give your life for another? What could be the only motivation? Write your thoughts in your journal.

Sacrifice To understand what Jesus really did for us and for all humanity, we need to appreciate what it means to offer sacrifice. Offering a sacrifice does not mean that we deprive ourselves of something. It is the offering of a gift. A *sacrifice* is a gift offered to God by a priest and destroyed in some way to show that it belongs to God alone. That is why the gift is burned or poured out or consumed. Offering a sacrifice is the highest form of worship that we can offer to God. How did this come to be?

Christ of Saint John of the Cross, Dalí, 1951

Ancient people thought that blood was the force of life. In Old Testament times our ancestors in faith thought the same way. They offered an animal in sacrifice to praise God and show their sorrow for sin. This sacrificial victim was killed on an altar, and its blood was poured out. In this way the ancient Jews believed that they were offering the gift of life itself back to the Giver of life. It would be God's forever, never to be taken back. The sacrifice was followed by a sacrificial meal. To eat this meal was to be in communion with God, who accepted the sacrifice and came among the people as they shared it.

The Passover Sacrifice

When offering a sacrifice, people gave only the best to God. They would offer their finest goat or calf, for example. At Passover an unblemished lamb was blessed and offered to God in sacrifice. The lamb was offered to God as a gift, as one of God's choicest creatures, both beautiful and innocent. Afterward all who shared in the Passover meal were united with one another and with Yahweh.

Passover was the celebration of Israel's "passing over" from slavery in Egypt to freedom, from death to life. During this celebration the Jews recalled all that God had done for them and God's saving and liberating activity in their history. At the first Passover it was the blood of the unblemished lamb that saved the firstborn children of Israel from death in Egypt. This made possible their departure for the promised land (Exodus 12:1–36).

Our Paschal Sacrifice   Jesus Christ is our Savior. He is our paschal, or Passover, lamb offered in sacrifice to the Father. At the crucifixion on Calvary, it was his blood, the blood of the Lamb of God, that saved all people from the death of sin and freed them for the promised land of heaven.

Jesus was the paschal victim like no other. Through him salvation and forgiveness of sins came to the whole world. In Jesus "we have redemption by his blood" (Ephesians 1:7). In the one sacrifice of the Lamb of God, the sacrifices of the old covenant came to an end. Jesus was both priest and victim on the altar of the cross; "he entered once for all into the sanctuary, not with the blood of goats and calves but with his own blood, thus obtaining eternal redemption" (Hebrews 9:12).

In the Old Testament there were many sacrifices offered daily in the Temple. In the New Testament there is only one sacrifice—the sacrifice in Jesus' blood. We now share in this one sacrifice at Mass. Christ does not die at each Mass, for death no longer has a hold over him; he has passed from death to risen and glorified life. Nevertheless the Mass is truly a sacrifice; it re-presents (makes present for us again) the one sacrifice of Calvary, prolonged in time. It is a perfect sacrifice: The victim is Christ; the priest is Christ. "The same Christ who offered himself once in a bloody manner on the altar of the cross is contained and offered in an unbloody manner" in the sacrifice of the Mass (*Catechism*, 1367).

Now that you know more about sacrifice and Jesus' passion and death, which part of the Mass has greater meaning for you?

 In reflecting upon the sacrifice of Jesus on the cross, the Church is reminded of the figure of the suffering servant. The prophet Isaiah described this servant as "pierced for our offenses" and taking upon himself "the guilt of us all." Isaiah also said that he was "like a lamb led to the slaughter" (Isaiah 53:5, 6, 7). That is why we call Jesus the Suffering Servant.

The New Covenant

Through Jesus' sacrifice on the cross, humanity has entered into a whole new relationship with God. We now have a new covenant established in the blood of Christ. What does this mean?

Long ago our ancestors in faith established a covenant, or agreement, with God on Mount Sinai. In this covenant they agreed to be God's chosen people, who would worship Yahweh as the one true God. Moses confirmed and sealed this covenant in Israel's name by sacrificing a lamb.

After the sacrifice was completed, Moses poured the lamb's blood on the altar. Then, following an ancient custom, he sprinkled some of the blood on the people assembled together. As he did this, he said, "This is the blood of the covenant which the LORD has made with you" (Exodus 24:8). Then the people ate the flesh of the lamb and were in communion with God and one another.

The covenant established at Sinai was the greatest event of the Old Testament. Through the laws of that covenant, God's people were formed and given life. The death and resurrection of Jesus are the greatest events in the New Testament. In them a new and everlasting covenant was confirmed and sealed, one that was made in Jesus' blood. Each time we participate in the Mass and share in the Body and Blood of Christ, the Lamb of God, we celebrate this new covenant and are in communion with God and one another.

Read again the words of Moses as he sprinkled the blood of the sacrificed lamb on the people. Now compare them with these words that we hear at each Mass: "Take this, all of you, and drink from it: this is the cup of my blood, the blood of the new and everlasting covenant. It will be shed for you and for all so that sins may be forgiven. Do this in memory of me." Both covenants were sealed in blood, but the new covenant was sealed in the blood of Christ.

Jesus, the Messiah, went beyond the expectations of all those around him. He rescued us from sin and brought salvation to everyone for all time. No one else could accomplish this. As we read in the Acts of the Apostles, "There is no salvation through anyone else, nor is there any other name under heaven given to the human race by which we are to be saved" (Acts 4:12).

The Resurrection

How can we be sure that the sacrifice of the cross brought us our salvation? We believe this because of Jesus' resurrection from the dead. As Paul declared, "If Christ has not been raised, then empty [too] is our preaching; empty, too, your faith" (1 Corinthians 15:14). The resurrection is the main reason for our faith in Christ: It completes Christ's sacrifice of love on the cross.

What was Jesus' resurrection like? We know that it was a real event, a historical fact. But it was more than the miracles that Jesus worked. Remember Jesus' friend Lazarus, whom Jesus raised from the dead. Jesus was not brought back only to an earthly life like Lazarus, so that he would have to die again. Jesus' resurrection was different: He was raised to *new life*. What does this mean?

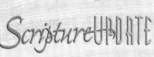

Scripture UPDATE

One of the most important titles for Jesus in the New Testament is Son of Man. In the gospel accounts this title is used only by Jesus when speaking of himself. Look up the following gospel passages in which *Son of Man* is used by Jesus, and see how rich and varied its many meanings are:

• Jesus referring to his human life (Luke 9:58)

• Jesus claiming divine powers (Mark 2:10)

• Jesus describing his mission (Luke 19:10)

• Jesus referring to his suffering and death (Mark 10:45)

• Jesus describing himself coming on the clouds of heaven as judge (Matthew 24:30–31). You may wish to read Daniel 7:13 in the Old Testament and compare both passages.

What will you think of the next time you hear *Son of Man* proclaimed at Mass?

This mystery of faith is never fully described in the gospels, but the testimony of eyewitnesses is clear. The risen Christ was seen and experienced by his followers. He ate with them and showed them his wounds. The risen body they saw was the same body that had been crucified and buried. Now risen, however, this real body had been totally transformed and was no longer subject to the laws of space and time. That is why the risen Jesus could pass through locked doors. In the gospels he is described as suddenly entering a locked room (John 20:19). We call the risen and transformed body of Christ his glorified body.

What does it mean for you to know that the risen Christ is with us today? Write your thoughts in your journal.

Things to SHARE

Share with your family and friends why it is so important for Christians to know about the Jewish Passover, the paschal lamb, the covenant at Sinai, and the offering of sacrifice. What do all these have to do with our salvation in Jesus Christ?

OnLine WITH THE PARISH

Arrange for your group to go on a "field trip" to your parish church. You will want to look especially at the altar, the vestments, and the sacred vessels used at the sacrifice of the Mass. See whether you can find any symbols that remind you of Jesus, the Lamb of God.

YOU ARE MY WITNESSES

Things to Think About

The apostle Thomas said he would not believe that Jesus was risen from the dead unless he could actually touch his wounds. Jesus said to him, "Blessed are those who have not seen and have believed" (John 20:29). Are you one of the "blessed"?

Why do you think Saint Paul said that our faith would be empty if Christ had not risen from the dead?

Words to REMEMBER

Find and define:

sacrifice

_____

_____

_____

_____

In The NaMe
Of the Father,
and of the Son,
and of the Holy Spirit.
Amen.

SIGN OF THE CROSS

GLoRy to the FaTHer,
AND TO THE Son,
and to the Holy Spirit:
as it was in the beginning, is now,
and will be for ever.
Amen.

GLORY TO THE FATHER

O My GoD,
I Firmly Believe that
you are one God in three divine
Persons, Father, Son, and Holy Spirit;
I believe that your divine Son
became man and died for our sins,
and that he will come to
judge the living and the dead.
I believe these and all the
truths which the holy
Catholic Church teaches,
because you revealed them,
who can neither deceive
nor be deceived. Amen.

ACT OF FAITH

CoMe, HoLy SpiRiT,
Fill the Hearts of your Faithful.
And kindle in them the fire of your love.

Send forth your Spirit and they shall be created.
And you will renew the face of the earth.

Let us pray.

Lord,
by the light of the Holy Spirit
you have taught the hearts of your faithful.
In the same Spirit
help us to relish what is right
and always rejoice in your consolation.

We ask this through Christ our Lord.
Amen.

PRAYER TO THE HOLY SPIRIT

EteRnaL ReSt
Grant unto Them,
O Lord.
And let perpetual light shine upon them.
May they rest in peace.
Amen.
May their souls and the souls of all the
faithful departed, through the mercy of
God, rest in peace.
Amen.

May the angels lead you into paradise;
may the martyrs come to welcome you
and take you to the holy city,
the new and eternal Jerusalem.

PRAYERS FOR THE DECEASED

O MY GOD, I LOVE YOU ABOVE ALL THINGS,

with my whole heart and soul,
because you are all good and worthy
of all my love. I love my neighbor
as myself for the love of you.
I forgive all who have injured me
and I ask pardon of all whom
I have injured. Amen.

ACT OF LOVE

O MY GOD, RELYING ON YOUR INFINITE

goodness and promises, I hope to
obtain pardon of my sins,
the help of your grace, and life
everlasting, through the merits
of Jesus Christ, my Lord and
Redeemer. Amen.

ACT OF HOPE

HAIL MARY, FULL OF GRACE,

the Lord is with you!
Blessed are you among women,
and blessed is the fruit of your womb,
Jesus.
Holy Mary, Mother of God,
pray for us sinners,
now and at the hour of our death.
Amen.

HAIL MARY

I BELIEVE IN GOD, THE FATHER ALMIGHTY,

creator of heaven and earth.
I believe in Jesus Christ, his only Son,
    our Lord.
He was conceived by the power of
    the Holy Spirit
    and born of the Virgin Mary.
He suffered under Pontius Pilate,
    was crucified, died, and was buried.
He descended to the dead.
On the third day he rose again.
He ascended into heaven,
    and is seated at the right hand
    of the Father.
He will come again to judge the living
    and the dead.
I believe in the Holy Spirit,
    the holy catholic Church,
    the communion of saints,
    the forgiveness of sins,
    the resurrection of the body,
    and the life everlasting.
    Amen.

APOSTLES' CREED

HAIL, HOLY QUEEN, MOTHER OF MERCY,

hail, our life, our sweetness, and our hope.
To you we cry, the children of Eve;
    to you we send up our sighs,
mourning and weeping in this land of exile.
Turn, then, most gracious advocate,
    your eyes of mercy toward us;
    lead us home at last
and show us the blessed fruit of your womb,
    Jesus:
O clement, O loving, O sweet Virgin Mary.

HAIL, HOLY QUEEN

WE BELIEVE IN ONE GOD,

THE FATHER, THE ALMIGHTY,

maker of heaven and earth,
of all that is seen and unseen.

We believe in one Lord, Jesus Christ,
the only Son of God,
eternally begotten of the Father,
God from God, Light from Light,
true God from true God,
begotten, not made, one in Being with
the Father.
Through him all things were made.
For us men and for our salvation
he came down from heaven:
by the power of the Holy Spirit
he was born of the Virgin Mary,
and became man.
For our sake he was crucified under
Pontius Pilate;
he suffered, died, and was buried.
On the third day he rose again
in fulfillment of the Scriptures;
he ascended into heaven
and is seated at the right hand of the
Father.
He will come again in glory to judge
the living and the dead,
and his kingdom will have no end.

We believe in the Holy Spirit, the Lord,
the giver of life,
who proceeds from the Father and the
Son.
With the Father and the Son he is
worshiped and glorified.
He has spoken through the Prophets.
We believe in one holy catholic and
apostolic Church.
We acknowledge one baptism for the
forgiveness of sins.
We look for the resurrection of the dead,
and the life of the world to come.
Amen.

NICENE CREED

JOYFUL MYSTERIES

1. The annunciation
2. The visitation
3. The nativity
4. The presentation
5. The finding of Jesus in the Temple

SORROWFUL MYSTERIES

1. The agony in the garden
2. The scourging at the pillar
3. The crowning with thorns
4. The carrying of the cross
5. The crucifixion

GLORIOUS MYSTERIES

1. The resurrection
2. The ascension
3. The coming of the Holy Spirit
4. The assumption of Mary
5. The coronation of Mary

MYSTERIES OF THE ROSARY

OUR FATHER,

WHO ART IN HEAVEN,

hallowed be thy name:
thy kingdom come;
thy will be done on earth as it is
in heaven.
Give us this day our daily bread;
and forgive us our trespasses
as we forgive those who trespass
against us;
and lead us not into temptation,
but deliver us from evil.
Amen.

OUR FATHER

P
R
A
Y
E
R
S

LORD, HAVE MERCY
LORD, HAVE MERCY

Christ, have mercy; Christ, have mercy
Lord, have mercy; Lord, have mercy

(The response to each of the
following is "Pray for us.")

Holy Mary, Mother of God
Saint Augustine
Saint Catherine
Saint Gregory
Saint Ignatius of Antioch
Saint John the Baptist
Saint Joseph
Saint Peter and Saint Paul
Saint Teresa
All holy men and women

SELECTIONS FROM THE LITANY OF SAINTS

MY GOD,
I AM SORRY FOR MY SINS WITH ALL MY HEART.

In choosing to do wrong
and failing to do good,
I have sinned against you
whom I should love above all things.
I firmly intend, with your help,
to do penance,
to sin no more,
and to avoid whatever leads me to sin.
Our Savior Jesus Christ
suffered and died for us.
In his name, my God, have mercy.

ACT OF CONTRITION

THE ANGEL SPOKE
GOD'S MESSAGE TO MARY,

and she conceived of the Holy Spirit.
Hail, Mary. . . .

"I am the lowly servant of the Lord:
let it be done to me according to your word."
Hail, Mary. . . .

And the Word became flesh
and lived among us.
Hail, Mary. . . .

Pray for us, holy Mother of God,
that we may become worthy of the
promises of Christ.

Let us pray.

Lord,
fill our hearts with your grace:
once, through the message of an angel you
revealed to us the incarnation of your Son;
now, through his suffering and death
lead us to the glory of his resurrection.
We ask this through Christ our Lord.
Amen.

THE ANGELUS

ALMIGHTY AND ETERNAL GOD,
YOU GATHER THE SCATTERED SHEEP

and watch over those you have gathered.

Look kindly on all who follow Jesus, your Son.
You have marked them with the seal of
one baptism,
now make them one in the fullness of faith
and unite them in the bond of love.
We ask this through Christ our Lord.
Amen.

PRAYER FOR UNITY

~ THE TEN ~ COMMANDMENTS

1. I am the Lord your God: you shall not have strange Gods before me.

2. You shall not take the name of the Lord your God in vain.

3. Remember to keep holy the Lord's Day.

4. Honor your father and your mother.

5. You shall not kill.

6. You shall not commit adultery.

7. You shall not steal.

8. You shall not bear false witness against your neighbor.

9. You shall not covet your neighbor's wife.

10. You shall not covet your neighbor's goods.

Catechism of the Catholic Church

~ THE ~ BEATITUDES

Blessed are the poor in spirit,
 for theirs is the kingdom of heaven.

Blessed are they who mourn,
 for they will be comforted.

Blessed are the meek,
 for they will inherit the land.

Blessed are they who hunger and thirst
  for righteousness,
 for they will be satisfied.

Blessed are the merciful,
 for they will be shown mercy.

Blessed are the clean of heart,
 for they will see God.

Blessed are the peacemakers,
 for they will be called children of God.

Blessed are they who are persecuted
  for the sake of righteousness,
 for theirs is the kingdom of heaven.

Matthew 5:3-10

Index

Italicized numbers refer to definitions   **Bold-faced** numbers refer to chapters